The Path Through Unhappiness To Happiness

This book tells how you can find a peace and happiness that will not leave you, even at moments when it seems that the entire world is against you. This book is for those who are searching for themselves, and who are prepared to take the great step of sacrificing the "I".

From the author:

In the first part of the book, I describe my life's path, which has much in common with that of many people who are just living their lives out to the end, whose lives are just dragging on. I use the specific phrase "dragging on" because few of us can confidently say – without it being a lie – that we are happy 24 hours a day. After all, we're used to seeing our lives the way we see a zebra – as black and white. Because of this, our happiness is temporary. It's dependent on external circumstances, and so, it's false happiness, not genuine. And this in spite of the fact that we humans have been given the unique opportunity to be truly happy our entire lives. In this book, I tell of my search for a happiness that is not fleeting, but rather, eternal and unshakeable.

The second, more practical section of the book tells how to control the disturbed, choppy mind that is the source of much of our suffering, and how to view all that happens in life with conscious perception.

Part I

The Beginning of the Search

> "Can one survive a month without food?"
> "Yes. But what about without meaning?"
> "Well, without meaning – you can live your whole
> life without that."

What do I want? What is it that I perpetually need? Why is it that I never leave myself in peace? Always demanding something of myself – feats of heroism, good behavior, right thoughts, a sense that I'm needed... a useful existence, love. I am so often dissatisfied with myself. Why? Why can't I live the way millions of others live. Wait a minute... Exactly how do they live? Maybe they live the same way I do, doubting, searching, finding and losing.

No, this senseless search for the meaning of life has to end. I need to just live, enjoy every moment and be joyful at each gulp of air I breathe in. But those are just words, empty words, as empty as life itself for the majority of homo sapiens. In reality, everything is much more complicated. These humdrum weekdays, rarely enriched by shopping trips or a perfectly grilled steak for breakfast. The same thing every day. Empty conversations, information-gathering, thoughts about your career, about sex; the exchange of pleasantries and games... nothing but games with both others and yourself.

That's how most people live, work, relax, travel, and then the cycle starts all over again. Really, people eat, they get drained of energy, then they eat again and are drained once more. In between, they exchange some phrases, have sex, bring children into the world, and then bring them up to be the same kind of biomasses as they themselves, the parents. But wait a minute, hold on... When children are born, it really does happen that a person awakens, opens its eyes for a brief moment, delighting that a new life has arisen, or, not delighting, as the case may be. And then that person drifts off to sleep again. And wakes up again only when it's time to give birth or die. And let's note that most people die like dogs, without ever having gotten around to considering the great secret of death. And all because of that sleep. It's like the famous Buddhist saying, "Wake up! It's time to die." In spite of this, sometimes our sufferings do wake us up. But we don't like suffering, we hate it and are terribly afraid of it. And not because we're forced out of our slumber against our will, but rather, because our self-esteem and our egotism are wounded, and because comparing ourselves with others really does us in. We think, why should I have to put up with that in my life? George over there, everything's going just great for him, but my life sucks. I'm so unhappy, so insulted by my fate, disillusioned with life. When this happens, a person is knocked out of his rut, and he does everything possible to climb right back into that rut. Without ever considering that maybe it was the rut itself that caused his problems in the first place. And it's good he doesn't think about that, because if he does, then he immediately blames himself and works himself up into a terrible feeling of guilt. I'm living wrong, my actions are wrong, my worldview is faulty. But I don't know how to live correctly, and so I suffer. And so you have a Catch-22. I begin to think about the causes of what happened – I blame myself, but don't really think it through, and end up making the same mistake again. What can you do? Really, in the large scheme of things, you don't need to do anything. Although comparing yourself to others is one good way to calm down and console yourself. We begin by calling to mind those who've found themselves in even worse situations than us, and then we say, "I'm doing okay. There are people who are a even worse off." These mind tricks definitely help, but only for a short while, and they only really help inveterate egotists.

At such times, people who've had some religious training and who know that dissatisfaction can be valuable, are more likely to turn to God and to try to accept what has happened with humility. These people became convinced as children that complaining about your fate is equivalent to angering God, because He will hear you and say, "You poor person, you still haven't learned how to live with unhappiness," and he'll send you an even more severe ordeal. But if you thank God for each minute of life, and if you remain happy, even when all crashes down around you, then God will say, "You poor person, you still haven't experienced true happiness. I'll send it to you so you can compare." Without a doubt, people who engage in religious thinking have an easier time of it than everyone else, because their faith strengthens them, helps them, and calms them. But there are treacherous currents here, too, namely blind exoteric faith and lack of faith.

It so happened that the Christian worldview became deeply rooted in me starting in my childhood. Maybe I got it from my grandmother, who had lived through World War II, lived long enough to see my wounded grandfather return from the front, and lost two brothers in that war. She prayed a lot before she went to bed, and before she ate, and she would go to church. She lived a long, difficult, and, I imagine, righteous, life. In her 80th year, she was still full of energy, hardly complained about anything except her hearing problems, weeded her garden very bit as well as the young folks, and would have nothing to do with television and the couch. But she died in her 90th year in total senility, smearing the walls of her room with excrement. I wouldn't really like to live that long... Thinking about the end of her life, I came to the conclusion that she had lived in total subjugation to her mind, totally in its control and under the sway of its turmoil, never free for a moment from this inner "monkey." And near the end, when she lost whatever weak control she'd had, then everything burst out. And I began to give it some thought. I asked myself, had her prayers been profound? Had she ever experienced peace? In other words, had she had true faith? It's my feeling that experiencing death in total non-awareness reduced her life to nothing. Of course, she left behind children and grandchildren (she added to the biomass,) planted a tree and built a house. But is this really the main goal of life on earth? If you don't get into questions about what each of us on earth is predestined to do, if you just live, then perhaps you could say that she did absolutely everything she was supposed to do. She fulfilled herself as a mother, a wife... she raised wonderful members of society, who in turn gave birth to other members. But if you talk about reaching a new level of consciousness, a profound level that separates us from animals (who also perpetuate the blood line and weave nests,) then her life's plan was a failure, as it is for the majority of us.

It just so happened that the orthodox religious education with which I was inoculated as a child has oppressed me my entire life. At first my faith was based mainly on terror. I'd hazard a guess (although I really hope I'm wrong about this) that this is the case with the majority of believers. You'll reach the heavenly kingdom if... You shouldn't sin, you do this or that... Observe the commandments, and you will be rewarded for your actions. My belief was strictly conditional. Religion placed too many conditions on me. We're all sinners and have been from birth. That's what was drummed into me by the religious books I read. This is what took firm root in my child's consciousness: don't sin, and you won't burn in hell. Only the righteous and those who repent end up in heaven. Unfortunately, that's exactly the way my understanding of religion started out,. Just like that. Later on, quite a lot in my religious views shifted. I came to understand that God is, first of all, great Love, and that you can discard everything else once you've gained this primary and core understanding. But my child's misunderstanding of how the world operates caused me a great deal of suffering in my adult life. Thinking about it now, I don't even know how this belief took root in me. My mother and father were communists, member of the Communist Party, and they paid no particular attention to questions of religion. You weren't supposed to be thinking about that. In the Soviet Union at that time, religion was strictly forbidden. Religious scholars are of the opinion that this actually saved religion in Russia, or more precisely, that it turned out to be a fortunate circumstance. The persecution of the church separated out the false believers. If you were a churchgoer, you could lose not only your job, but your life. So, only the true believers went to church, those for whom everything else but God – including their own lives – was secondary. My grandmother didn't talk with me much about religion, never invited me to pray with her, and never pressured me to go to church. I enjoyed listening to how she spoke to God, and I knew the Our Father practically from the time I was in diapers. But it wasn't until much later that I learned that God never punishes, that God always loves, and that the only sin on earth is a lack of love. But by the time I found that out, I'd already made more than a few mistakes. Actually, I still make them. But there aren't so many of them, and they don't have such awful consequences as they used to. And they're not mistakes any more – now I call them small missteps.

You pay a high price for truth. Sometimes we pay for it with our health, or suffering, or failures. But it's all worth it, because in return we gain wisdom, and over time, that wisdom becomes priceless. Maybe there are some people who can learn wisdom from reading smart books, who can learn from others' experience, others' mistakes. I don't know any people like that, though. My path, my search for myself, was torturous, thorny, difficult, and full of victims. We all learn however we can. I read in some book about biology that smart animals learn after doing something three times, dumb ones after seven. We need only trace the course of our lives and look at our usual pattern of mistakes to be convinced that this is true. Our mistakes are basically the same. Only the conditions, surroundings and reasons change. Recall your own life, and take a look at a few of the painful moments. If you fall into the same pit three times and then see the pit before you step into it, then congratulations! You're one of the smart ones. If it takes you seven times, you've got some work ahead of you. But it's never too late to learn. I usually have to do things three times before I see that I've been through the same thing before. Oh, these situations can drag out for years. Let's say I did something, and received some material benefit or some pleasure from it. Then in a year a similar situation comes along and I go for it again, and then, after some time goes by, it happens yet again. And then suddenly I see that I'm headed in the wrong direction and doing the exact opposite of what I need to be doing. And so I reject that approach and start over again, from the beginning. I'm really glad that I'm able to see I'm getting nowhere after three failures, and not seven. Maybe there really are people who get it the first time around. But I'm not one of them. I know more than a few people who don't reflect at all on their mistakes in life. They just go with the flow. Is that a good thing? Sure, as long as you don't get to thinking about the meaning of life and asking yourself that kind of question. For example, one of my friends has been married four times, and if you ask me, all four of the men she chose are like Xerox copies of each other, all of absolutely the same psychological type. Meanwhile, each time, my friend asserts, no, this one isn't like the last one, they're as different as day and night. They look different, and their mannerisms are different, and really, there's not an iota of similarity between this one and the last. But the ending is pathologically identical: a female heart gets broken yet one more time. This example reminds me of an old and not entirely kind joke. One friend says to the other: I don't have any luck with men. The first one and I broke up because he slapped me; the second hit me in the face and I couldn't forgive him, and now it's the same thing with the third one. And the friend says to her, "Well, if all three of them have aimed at your face, it means there's something about your face that's asking for a brick to be thrown at it." Evidently my friend will learn her life's lesson after the seventh time. What can you do? Each person has his own path.

All the same, it is possible for people who go with the flow without reflecting much on the meaning of life to be totally happy, but only just from time to time. Because we all have our own buckets of tears and sufferings. And this is one of the wisdom's of life that we all have to learn: life contains suffering. For this reason, there's no point in comparing the size of your bucket of tears with your neighbor's, because one person might have fewer tears, but they're more bitter, and another person might have more tears, but they're sweeter. Everyone wants to avoid suffering in life, but in the process they end up suffering more. Do people really have the power to avoid suffering or to minimize it? Does man truly forge his own fate, or is that just an illusion? Or maybe everything is predestined to such a degree that it doesn't make sense to even try. Maybe we're only little worker ants who consider ourselves kings? Or perhaps we really are kings dragging out the miserable lives of slaves? Dragging out our lives this way because we don't know our potential. Or maybe we have no potential? Maybe all we have are the pointless attempts of philosophers to discover happiness. I suggest that you, the reader, and I try to answer this question together. I'll lay out several currently existing theories that partially answer these questions. Who are we and why are we here? To suffer or to experience pleasure? To be kings or slaves? To moan with pleasure every day or to be tortured in agony by unhappiness and misfortune?

Hardship and Casting About

A man is tossing and turning, unable to fall asleep, all the while wondering, does God exist or not... Suddenly a voice rings out: "I don't exist! Now go to sleep!"

My religious upbringing which, as I noted at the beginning, was faulty, led me to a moment in life when I was forced to consider whether all I'd absorbed since I was a child was correct. Whether it's right to live with one eye always on the fear instilled in me by religion. The fear of committing a sinful, wrong or unwise act. The fear of appearing guilty or foolish in the eyes of society. This fear, plus what my mind saw as a close connection between crime and punishment, finally led to a point where I was living in total exhaustion. By age thirty I was so petrified that I was simply scared to live. It's even difficult to find a word that would accurately describe my inner state at that moment. It was a state of feeling crushed, frightened, doomed, despondent, and unable to enjoy life. I understood full well that this mental state hadn't arisen overnight, but was rather the result of a character that had developed over the course of thirty years. At its core lay a flawed worldview and, to some extent, my incorrect interpretation of the Christian picture of the world, which centered around the problem of sin. For example, if there was something I wanted to do, I mean, really wanted to do, something which Christian dogma would view as a sin, I would usually say to myself, I'm being tested. From there, my thought process would usually go like this: I need to work on myself more, try to renounce worldly temptations, work more on my spirituality. I would recall wise biblical sayings such as "All is allowed, but not everything is beneficial, all is permitted, but nothing should possess me." "Rich is not he who has more, but he who needs less." But none of this mental activity brought the necessary result. If there was something I really, really wanted, desire just erupted. And if, after carefully weighing all the pros and cons, I nonetheless allowed myself to act on my desire, gave myself "permission," and consequently received a certain dose of normal human pleasure (which many even call happiness,) then afterwards I'd involuntarily experience such a feeling of guilt that I just couldn't free myself from it. It even got to the point that if something unpleasant happened not long afterwards, my mind would suddenly say, "that's what you get." It's difficult to imagine how strongly my lack of love for myself was at those moments. I'd reached the end of my rope because of my approach to life. I began to be afraid of living. I began to be afraid of having to pay for my sins. I had no real idea how to live, how to live correctly. I was tormented by the connection between crime and punishment, by thoughts about what constitutes a sin and what doesn't, about whether I was repentant, and sincerely. Is the answer that a person should move toward complete freedom from dogma, prejudice, of persistent sin? I didn't get why, from the Christian perspective, man is sinful. Who the hell thought that up? I didn't get it, but all the same I kept believing it. I continued rummaging around in various religions, searching for answers. I explored nearly all the world religions, seeking answers to the multitude of questions which, by the time I turned thirty, had overtaken my disturbed mind to such an extent that it was becoming more and more difficult to live in society.

Orthodox Christianity

I absorbed Orthodoxy from the time I was little. This was faith in the holy trinity, belief in physical resurrection, the ascension, and the second coming of Christ, and universal resurrection. Plus the commandments that every Christian knows: You shall have no other gods before me, you shall not make any graven images, or take the name of the Lord in vain. Honor the Sabbath, honor your father and mother; do not kill, do not commit adultery, do not steal, do not bear false witness, do not covet your neighbor's house or your neighbor's wife, or his ox.

Protestantism
This is one of the three main branches of Christianity (together with Orthodoxy and Catholicism.) Over the course of the past two years, I made an effort to understand and embrace Protestantism, but finally understood that my path lay elsewhere.

In Protestantism, one's soul is saved through faith in Jesus Christ as one's personal savior, and through God's grace, which manifested in the fact that Jesus died for the sins of each person. (Catholics and Orthodox Christians reject this point.) Protestantism also preaches about the Trinity of God, about the immortality of the soul, about heaven and hell (and rejects the Catholic teaching about Purgatory.) Protestants believe that one can receive forgiveness for one's sins through belief in Jesus Christ (i.e., through believing that he died for the sins of everyone, and that he rose from the dead.)

Jehovah's Witnesses
I got to know Jehovah's Witnesses because I wanted to learn about all forms of religion. Jehovah's Witnesses entirely reject the existence of the soul, spirits or any

other non-material essences. They believe in eliminating what they call the currently existing "system of things" and in the creation of a heaven on Earth that will exist eternally. Over the 1000 years after Armageddon a great resurrection will take place, and in the course of this resurrection, the majority of those who have lived on Earth will be restored to life. Jehovah's Witnesses consider fornication a grave sin, and for them, any sexual relations between unmarried people fall into that category. Masturbation and watching pornography, etc., are considered "impure" acts and are also condemned. They categorically refuse to take part in political or military action. They use alcohol in moderation. They strive for modesty in their dress and adornments. Jehovah's Witnesses pray only to Jehovah in the name of Jesus Christ. They fully reject any spilling of blood. And like representatives of the majority of Christian churches, they see the Bible as the sole basis for their dogma. So, they do not accept the Trinity.

It's interesting that the members of each religious group, whether they're Protestants, Jehovah's Witnesses, or Catholics, interpret the Bible in their own way, and all of them assert that their views are based exclusively on the truth of the Bible. And they can easily prove any of their positions with the help of Bible verses. I still find this incomprehensible. Either it's because they use a special translation that's matched to their teachings, or they manage to read the verses in such a way that you'll see in them precisely what the teachings are preaching.

Jainism
Jainism originated in India. The goal is to free oneself from karma and reach nirvana in one's lifetime. The

Jains believe one can do this through strict asceticism. The main commandments are: to harm no living being, to be honest, to not steal, to not covet, to never steal things which belong to others or which they've lost, and to not acquire material wealth. The biggest sin for them is to harm another living being. For this reason, adherents of Jainism generally don't move around at night, so that they don't crush an ant or spider by accident.

Buddhism
I understand all that Buddhism preaches, and it resonates with me. I love this religion and accept it fully. It's the most ancient of all existing religions, and it, too, came from India. Buddhism as I understand it, is the path of the middle-way warrior. Buddha left the path of full asceticism, since he understood the futility of that approach, and at the same time he warned of the dangers of attachment to material things. He urged people to find the golden middle path between these two extremes and to follow it. The Four Noble Truths which the Buddha formulated have to do with suffering. He considers the causes of suffering (sickness, old age and death) and offers a path each person can follow to end his suffering. His Eightfold Path requires wisdom, morality and spiritual discipline. Its main points are fairly simple: all things are impermanent, all beings suffer from a "obscured" mind, and that the sense of a permanent "self" is an illusion. The Buddha's Eightfold Path gives a detailed description of each step of spiritual development. On the last step one's consciousness is liberated and, as a result, suffering disappears, and one experiences complete joy and tranquility. Just as is the case with Christianity, there are more than twenty branches of Buddhism, various schools which preach

differing paths of spiritual development, but the goal of all of them is the same: enlightenment.

Advaita

I became acquainted with this Indian philosophical movement in Russia. One of the contemporary teachers of Advaita is Cesar Teruel. He travels the cities of the worlds offering free satsangs during which one can achieve awakening. These satsangs actually "pierce" the consciousness of the person who is ready for transformation. I myself have witnessed the unbelievable metamorphosis of people who received from Cesar the very thing for which they'd been waiting their entire lives.

Advaita asserts the non-duality of the world and the absence of any duality at all. True reality is recognized as emptiness. Our suffering is a total illusion. In reality, people already possess happiness and liberation, they're already saved. But the main obstacle to grasping this truth lies in our mind. In Advaita there's an understanding of three levels of reality: the paramarthika (true reality), viarvakhrikha (conventional reality, which means our material world,) and the pratibkhasikha (transparent reality, such as our dreams.) The main Advaita text is the Upanishads. Advaita destroys our familiar way of thinking, destroys our emotional mind, i.e., ignorance, and reveals the path to liberation. Advaita is a pretty interesting philosophical trend. Partly with the help of an awakened Master, people can achieve a state of consciousness in which only the functional mind is present, the mind which enables one to exist in the real world. But the emotional mind, which is our main obstacle to finding truth, is absent. It's the emotional mind that compares, judges, seeks benefit, and so on. In its absence, life becomes joyous, and suffering disappears.

Kabbalah

I haven't studied Kabbalah in depth. To my mind it has something in common with Buddhism. It's a current of Judaism that studies the Torah, which contains all the information about our world. Those who study Kabbalah feel that the source of all mankind's problems is that we don't live in a way that's compatibility with the laws of the universe. According to Kabbalah, the soul manifests in the material world until such time as it "learns its lessons" and fulfills the function for which it was created. When one achieves this goal – by studying Kabbalah – the soul will stop taking material form. Another goal of Kabbalah is to gain deeper understanding of the laws of life and of the world. This knowledge makes it possible for people to approach life properly.

New Age

It's hard to call this a religious movement, since there are no specific concepts associated with it. Rather, it encompasses several spiritual teachings. I've never considered myself part of the New Age movement, but I fully accept all of its ideas. I like the works of Steiner, Osho, Gurdjieff, and Sai Baba, who in recent times have begun to be considered New Age. Of course these great modern figures never belonged to any organizations or groups. They were just people of this planet. They're lumped in with New Age mainly because of their innovative and fresh ideas about how to harmonize human development. The New Age movement sees the founders of the world's religions, and their prophets – Christ, Buddha, Mohammed and others – as people who achieved the highest levels of awakening. New Age followers are united by their search for awakening, and a general belief in love and the unity of all that exists. They recognize no divisions between religions, they believe in rebirth and karma, and tend toward ecumenicalism. In their view, each person is capable of rising to the highest levels (achieving "Christ consciousness".)

Zen

Zen Buddhism adheres to the concept of instant enlightenment, in which an adept is able to realize cosmic reality in one instant. In some sense, Zen arose as a protest against the idea of gradual enlightenment. Zen Buddhists say one can achieve enlightenment in this lifetime. Even so, for some people, instantaneous enlightenment isn't necessarily simpler or easier to achieve than gradual. Those who have "weak roots" (i.e., those who aren't spiritually ripe,) might never experience it, even if they've pursued spiritual development in the course of many lifetimes. For these people gradual enlightenment might be more suitable. This approach includes adhering to precepts such as developing charity and love; studying the scriptures; and praying to be reborn in higher spiritual realms so as to be able to progress along the path to enlightenment. Once one attains an elevated or deepened state through meditation, one begins to perceive reality differently. For Zen Buddhists, this is the experience of seeing one's true "I". Really, this investigation of one's true nature is the basis of Zen. If unrealized desires serve as the basis for suffering, then the way to free oneself from internal tension is to realize them. After all, it's this tension, this dissatisfaction with how things have turned out in life that constitutes suffering. But since no one can realize all their desires, you have to distinguish the ones you can realize from those it's impossible or really difficult to realize. It's a clear and simple idea: you have to either realize desires, if that's possible, or else free yourself from them, and just forget about them. Within Zen, there's no other path to inner liberation. One way to express this idea is with the phrase "Relax and all will come." The practice and study of Zen are focused on calming the soul, on freeing the mind from minor desires, on liberation from harsh views and unnecessary attachments. This practice makes it more likely that one will be able to glimpse one's self-nature, an experience that is free of all practice and all paths.

Faith

Atheism class. The teacher says,
"Children. There is no God! You there, Mary, can
you see God?"
"No."
"So what does that tell you?"
"That there is no God!"
At this point Bobby, in the back row, raises his hand.
The teacher asks,
"Bobby. Do you have something to add?"
"Mrs. Johnson, may I ask Mary a question?"
"Go ahead."
"Mary, can you see Mrs. Johnson's brains?"
"No."
"So what does that tell you?"

I want to stress that I had never considered the question of faith. My faith was never in doubt, no matter what situations life brought me. I was and have remained a person of deep faith. I never renounced my faith. I only sought to take another look at my religious views, since at the moment I was experiencing a whole bunch of doubts.

Through my work as well as through my own search for truth, I came into contact with a huge number of representatives of various religious faiths, ranging all the way from Orthodox priests and Catholics to Buddhists, Muslims and Jehovah's Witnesses. And each religious branch had its share of differences of opinions. All Christians rely on one main text – the Bible, but they read it in various ways. Some interpret it practically literally, while others go so deeply into complicated explanations that, try as you might, you can't understand them. But even if you're a reader with little experience with religious literature, you'll see right away that the ideas that separate the various schools diverge so insignificantly, and the differences are so superficial that they really aren't worth worrying about. For example, should one observe on Saturday or Sunday; what name should we use for God; when should we fast, and how many times a day should we pray? It seems to me that how profound one's faith is really has nothing to do with these questions. The common ground is that the basic, deep postulates of all religions are similar. You can find parallels and find much in common between the Vedas, the Koran, the Bible, and other sources. So, when the time came in my life when I began to experience what psychology calls personal growth, and when I posed the question that every thinking person asks himself sooner or later – where to head next – it so happened that that darn underlying religious education of mine asserted itself. It's hard to free yourself from sin when you've been told from the time you were a child that you're sinful, that you were born in sin. Christ atoned for the sins of humanity, showed us the way, taught us to prepare for the Heavenly Kingdom. If you ask what they mean by "Heavenly Kingdom," the Evangelicals start talking to you vaguely about eternal life in heaven and about the delightful existence that awaits you in exchange for living a righteous life. It's all in vague terms because everything we know about eternal life is purely theoretical – no one has yet reached the Heavenly Kingdom, and we know of it only from generally accepted teachings of the church that puts them forth. And so it turned out that my first timid attempt to free myself from religious dogma and to begin to acquainting myself with the truths of life not through a religious prism, but rather through my own experience, without having anything foisted upon my by anyone else – that attempt was a total failure. My religious worldview was simply too strong. I was caught in an endless loop, always ending up where I'd started out, turning again and again to the path of repentance and acceptance.

I took a look at my life and came to the conclusion that I had earned everything I'd been given. That I really was sinful, that I have my cross to bear, and that that cross, by the way, isn't really all so heavy compared to the crosses of others who are trudging through life. I concluded that I shouldn't try to make things better for myself, that you can't avoid suffering anyway, that like it or not, the truth is hidden from simple mortals. I wouldn't be able to grasp it. And so, yet one more time, I chose the path of the sheep, rather than the shepherd, for I had no idea where to head. But this was the path of a clever sheep. I simply placed responsibility for all my decisions on God. If He let me take those steps, then He was responsible. Even so, I was every bit as far as I'd been before from solving the questions of love, compassion and openness toward people. All I'd done was to gain some inner calm and find myself a comfortable spot. In other words, I got myself a new trough, got into it, and set off through the very same swamp as before. And I really did feel better. I calmed down, gave up the soul searching, and stopped chastising myself for living wrong (I've always had the sense I was living wrong,) for the fact that I can't be happy (I was always fixated on searching for happiness, even though at that time it seemed to those around me that I was a successful businesswoman, a young mother, a beloved wife.) Many people openly envied me, and when I'd make my timid attempts to escape my routine or change something in my life, they'd say, she's spoiled, what else does she need? She has a great job, her husband simply adores her, she has kids. And at some point, I gave in and adopted everyone else's way of seeing things. I stopped looking for happiness, rooting around in cause and effect, searching for an answer to the philosophical question of who I am and why I'm here. I began to just live, without trying to answer these questions that seemed impossible to answer. I began to live, moving along my familiar, totally comfortable, everyday life's path. I turned my back on the past without giving much thought to the value of the present, thinking about the future no differently than the way most people on earth do.

Did things get easier for me, more peaceful? To a certain degree, yes. But not for long. Things got a little more comfortable. I stopped rushing around, settled down, went back to my family. I'll say that this search for myself complicated things between my husband and me for a long time. I'd be searching, tear off in one direction, I would always be unhappy with something or other. At first I tried filling up the space with Qigong. A week-long seminar in the capital, hour-long morning meditations. Total failure. I understood that it wasn't for me, that I wasn't into it, that I was just running away from something. Then there was my Lazarev period – complete with his seminars in various world cities, CDs, books, consultations. Then it was Agni Yoga. I made several other unsuccessful attempts to find myself. I got nowhere. They were all nothing more than attempts to escape something, primarily myself. I was deeply unhappy about something, but I couldn't get a clear sense of what it was. Finally I began to blame my husband for all my troubles. The thought crept into me that I didn't love him, and that that was the source of all my problems. I suddenly understood that I was living with a person with whom I had nothing in common, and that I'd been living with him nearly 20 years. I have to give my husband credit – at first he tried his best to explain the way things were to me, using other families as an example. Look how everyone else lives, he'd say. Everyone's in the same boat. Every couple argues, makes up, lives through crises. What kind of love are you talking about, he'd ask me. Love passes, and what takes its place is taking care of each other and the kids, raising them. And by the way, in Japanese, the phrase "I love you" means "I take care of you." We're living like 96% of all other families, he'd tell me. To which I'd respond that I wanted to live like the other five percent, I wanted my marriage to be one of the ones made in heaven. I didn't want to be amongst the gray masses living without love. I didn't want to live with my husband just because we had kids together, only because it was easier or more comfortable or convenient that way, or only because the kids needed a father. My husband accepted my attempts to find myself with relative calm, but near the end his nerves couldn't take it. Who could stand that? But that happened right at the point when I was the most disappointed in myself. I decided to stop the search and just live, just live the way I knew how to live. I understood that there was nothing I could change in my wheel of life, that it would keep turning just the same way it had been set spinning many years earlier. I saw that all the efforts I'd made were like running pointlessly in this wheel of life, while thinking that I had control over everything. But if you just drop everything, the momentum will carry you forward for a long time. Is there any point in fighting windmills and pretending to be Don Quixote? I made the decision to abandon all attempts to uncover the truth. I began living like millions of other people all over the world. I began to live the way I knew how, or more precisely, in the way that was most convenient for me.

The Right Direction

The path leads to nowhere. The main thing is not to go astray.

I stopped terrorizing my husband and stopped expressing my dissatisfaction with myself and my life. I calmed down and turned my attention back to work, to everyday matters, to spending time with my friends. I just gave up the struggle, because I understood that if you're living in a dualistic state – as modern people do – it's impossible to find truth. Until you attain a different state of consciousness, no guidelines will work right, there's no formula you adopt will be effective, and no laws of the world or wisdom will bear fruit. I couldn't attain that state, so why torment myself further? Oh, and by the way, all my friends came to the conclusion that I was now on the right track. They began turning to me more and more often as a confidante, as a psychologist, or simply as a shoulder to cry on. They'd often call and confide in me about their personal business, or ask for advice, saying, you know so much, you always know how to approach things. And I, naively assuming that I really did know something and could help in some way, would give some really primitive advice about how my friends could fix their lives, or change themselves, or improve their character. I spent nearly two years in this state of sleep, falsehood and fleeting peace. Everyone was happy about that, including my husband. It was convenient and comfortable for everyone. I'd be lying if I said that during those two years I never entertained thoughts about divorce and freedom, about the meaning of life and whether I was in the right place for me, whether I was moving in the right direction. Sure, I went there, numerous times. But each time I worked out way to keep those thoughts at bay. I'd forbid myself to have doubts about this or that. I'd reassure myself: I'm doing everything right, I'm in the right place, I've kept my family together, I have a good marriage, we have a normal family. I've planted trees and now I'm tending the garden of my life. And really, searching for truth is a male path, the prerogative of the strong sex, while feminine spirituality, what does that mean? There hasn't even been much written about it, since not much of anyone has been very interested in it. The woman is always more concrete – her destiny is to bear children, educate them, take care of the family hearth, create comfort. What, do I need something more than everyone else? I have that hearth and it's my job to take care of it. And so I threw myself into that job with my usual fervor. We started taking family picnics more often, spending more time with each other. I pushed away any doubts that periodically came into my head about whether I was living the right way. I didn't allow any doubts in - there had been way too many of them before. And they hadn't led to anything good. Only to breakdowns, hopelessness and empty acts. And so, the hell with it, I decided. We were given commandments two thousand years ago. Ten of them. That's the simplest path. And by the way, this always reminds me of a joke: Moses comes down to the people after his discovery and says, "I have good news and I have bad news. Which do you want to hear first?" And the people say, "Start with the good news." "Okay," says Moses.

"There are fewer commandments now. Just ten." The people give a sigh of relief. "Here's the bad news: adultery is still included."

At that point my religious mind reasoned, Christ instructed us to go along the straight and narrow. It's a simple path, and you can't get lost on it, but it's definitely more complicated to follow. There's another path, a wider one, one that has a bunch of temptations. That one's easier to follow because many have followed it, and you'll always have jolly company on your way, because it's the path most people choose. I'm not going to look for some third path. That leaves two, and they were described way back in the Bible. So, let's look at the wide path. It's interesting, of course, but it's not the one for me, since I've already spent quite a bit of time on it. By now I'd already partly traveled the path of Zorba. And as I've already written, nothing grew for me along that path except for a feeling of guilt. That leaves that "right" biblical path, based solely on observing the ten commandments. And so, I pulled in my oars. I wasn't going to reach enlightenment. Zorba's path no longer interested me, and the Buddha's was unattainable. What was left was just to live as I knew how to live. So, I became a "good girl," a faithful and correct wife who no longer strived for enlightenment, an attentive mother. True, from time to time I'd drink myself unconscious with my girlfriends, without even knowing why *they* were drinking. *I* drank out of weakness, because I wasn't able to be honest with myself. Who knows why they drank. But we all have our own demons in our head that we have to drive out every once in a while. Psychologists refer to this as deadening our crazy-making super ego by means of alcoholism.

Probably, this was how I relieved stress. But whatever the case, I stayed with my husband. That was the key thing. At least that's what everyone around me – including myself – thought. And at that point I thought I'd made the right choice. I kept the family together, protecting those closest to me from worrying about the wife who was off searching for who knows what and who knows why.

And so it was inevitable that what happened happened. All of a sudden our family ship hit the rocks and began to sink.

In a Fit of Passion

"Babaji, am I living correctly?"
"Yes... but in vain."

A question to consider: does a wife have the right to leave her husband? Not a husband who's a despot or an alcoholic or a drug addict or who likes the fast life. But one who's a good person in every regard. Judging by commentaries on the Bible, no. If the husband gives the wife a divorce and she unites her life with another – then it's adultery. If the husband leaves her for someone else, that's adultery, too. Of course, you can't interpret the Bible purely literally. And of course, it was written a thousand years ago and intended for people with a slightly different consciousness. At that time there was a need for a code of rules to keep people in line. But now our thinking and consciousness have evolved. We understand and realize more. Through the tens and hundreds of enlightened people who've been born in various periods, we've gained some knowledge about how the world is structured. Biblical truth is profound and multifaceted, but you have to search for it, because it's encoded. On the most superficial levels, the majority of biblical chapters are so identical and straightforward, that if you have an ordinary worldly, materialistic outlook, and you're looking for some other, hidden meaning in them, it's like trying to catch a fish from an ocean beach. It's also useless to attempt this if you're someone who learned from the time you were little that all you need to do is unquestioningly follow everything written in the Bible, that it's sacred, and that this is the code of rules by which a true Christian should be guided. Well, it just so happened that I violated one of the most important commandments. In our family

28

there occurred a betrayal. It's not so interesting how it happened. I'll just say that it was a stormy romance, full of passion. In the course of fifteen years of marriage, I hadn't experienced sexual attraction to my husband. I was ashamed to even admit this to myself. But in eastern countries, it's not customary for spouses to discuss this kind of thing. Besides which, for women this is not considered problematic. After all, you don't need an orgasm to bear children. I knew I wasn't frigid. The problem lay in my relationship with my husband. After all, orgasm is always in your head. Anatomically, any woman can have one. On a purely physiological level, men can reach orgasm with any woman, but it's more complicated for women. Women experience orgasm only with someone with whom she can be open on three levels: physically, mentally, and spiritually. If any of these are blocked – no orgasm. I had an inkling that some block of this kind was present in my head, but I couldn't do anything about it. Sex was routine. So in my case, betraying my husband was a chance for me to change something in my life and to learn more about myself. The two of us found each other interesting. We were so overcome by passion that whenever we'd meet, we were ready to rip each other's clothes off, we could hardly restrain ourselves. Luckily, the whole thing didn't last long. It took such a terrible toll on me. Every time I met him, I'd blossom, and every time I crossed the threshold of my own house, I'd droop.

A love triangle is one of the most serious tragedies that can befall a person. The triangle destroys everything: your health, your relationships, your love. Speaking from my own experience, I can say with total certainty, that the unhappiest woman is the one who has a lover. I think that applies to men, too. But let's face it – men are less susceptible to worrying about things like guilt. Men have a clearer idea of who they love versus who they're just sleeping with, so love triangles aren't as disastrous as they are for women. More often than not, a woman loves every man she sleeps with, except in rare cases – we're not taking chance sexual encounters into account here. So, things are usually mixed up in the female brain. She has a harder time distinguishing between pure physical attraction and being in love. Besides, since time immemorial, women have had it drummed into their heads that their sexuality can't equal men's, that women express their sexuality less and that it's physically weaker. But in actual fact, women are polygamous, just like men. They're just as sexually interested in their partners as are men. The feminine nature needs sex just as much and also has an appetite for sexual contact. What's different is that in women, it's all a bit closed off. It's closed off by her feeling of shame (another behavior imposed on her by society.) She fashions herself into some kind of bait for the man to go for, and plays a game: I'm the prey, you're the hunter. That's the way it's been seen for hundreds of years. But in reality, the woman can be the hunter, too, and can experience sexual hunger and chase men. But while the chase is on, the woman's more likely to naively think that she loves this man, and that that's why she wants him. It isn't at all that she just wants him, but later on maybe she'll come to love him. On the subconscious level, the goal is the same – to have her eggs fertilized and reproduce, to continue the race. Reproducing is one of the basic instincts of any woman. Married or not. Of course, the only difference is that an unhappily married woman is looking for a better match, while a single woman is looking for a match, period.

A lover's triangle provides serious motivation for taking a good look at your life. This geometric figure indicates a lack of love in the family. It arises at the very point when the ship is already sinking. It appears so that it can either sink the ship or save it. Unfortunately, experience shows that more often than not, the ship sinks. The only ships that can't be sunk are the unsinkable ones, and it's hard to get close to such a vessel. If a woman's happily married and loves her husband, then it's unlikely anyone will be able to catch her eye. The most you'll get if this is the case is a little flirting. The same is true with men. But there is a small percentage of cases when a love triangle can actually resuscitate a relationship. But triangles can serve as a restorative medicine only in open marriages. And this can only happen when a man and a woman are able to talk openly about their problems, when they're capable of working together to find a solution, and of forgiving each other deeply in the process. You'll agree that there aren't too many couples like that. What happens most often is that the woman will either try to forget what drew her to another's bed, will hide it and carry on with her life with her husband with a huge sense of guilt, or she'll leave him.

In our family we never had an open relationship. Trusting, friendly, partner-like, yes, but not open. I wasn't capable of having a discussion with my husband about what I didn't like about our life together. It's not acceptable for us to talk about our sexual life, or about how we feel about each other. I can't tell my husband there's something in our sex life I don't like, because he'll be deeply wounded by that. I'm not capable of making changes in that area, because a host of suspicions would arise. And he's incapable of forgiving infidelity. I even doubt that he could live through that.

His indescribable jealous has been a part of our life from the time we first met, even though there was no particular basis for it. I got used to it and it didn't particularly bother me. But intuitively I knew that if my husband even thought I might be seeing someone else, he was capable of killing me, literally. His pride, arrogance, sense of his own worth and his insane jealousy made it impossible for me to open up to him and share my concerns. That would have hurt him emotionally, and would probably have ruined his health, too. I really did not want to hurt him, and so my complaints piled up, and my little bundle of problems grew steadily larger and larger. And still I couldn't say anything about them, because I was afraid of hurting him, and afraid of losing the chance to raise my children. What's more, I'm from an eastern country where people have fairly strict views. My husband has pretty firm convictions on this score: a wife who strays has no right to raise her children. For better, or perhaps for worse, I broke things off with the man, since this fleeting romance totally exhausted me. Once again I became convinced that I was incapable of loving my husband, and not only that, but incapable of loving anyone but myself. This both tormenting and pleasant period of passion, of forbidden desires and love (or false love) totally wrung me out. At that point, I thought of love as the desire to care for someone, to be with him for the rest of my life, to be totally open with him, to dissolve into him, and of course, it goes without saying, that I'd never think of looking for someone else. Unfortunately, most people straddle the fence on this point. They live with their partners, but at the same time, they're looking for someone else, and if a good opportunity arises, they'll switch partners. Not many people have the nerve to say, "I don't love you any more. Goodbye."

And it isn't even so much that they don't have the nerve, as that people can't figure themselves out and are unable to understand what love is. If someone leaves a marriage, it's usually because of a love triangle. In most cases, people spend days, months, and years living with spouses they don't love. They say they're doing it out of habit, or convenience, and they justify it by saying that they have children, and that the children should grow up in an intact family. I was no exception.

Throughout all these years of rather primitive day-to-day interactions with my husband, I was sitting on the fence. I played the role of the happy wife, enjoyed the status of a married woman, but at the same time I was accumulating a pile of complaints toward my husband. I allowed them to pile up silently. We so totally bought into this image of ourselves as a cultured couple, living peacefully and happily, raising two charming children, that we even stopped expressing our emotions openly. We almost never argued, especially in front of the children. We accepted each other's existence and each other's faults. I don't know whether I should really say "we", since I don't know how my husband experienced it. But as far as I'm concerned, my insincerity in regard to him had reached such a low point that my life with him turned into a cold civil war. There was no open warfare. How could there be, when there were so many witnesses around: relatives, friends, neighbors. We were masters at playing the role of the happy husband and wife. But our complaints remained. Our outwardly decorous existence ate away at me inside. There was a lot about my husband that annoyed me. The thought that I didn't love him had taken root in me so deeply that I was ready to leave at any moment. But how? How could I explain to everyone around me that I just didn't love my husband?

That I didn't love such a kind, caring, hard-working, wonderful father. How can you leave someone like that? And besides, on the outside we had a very good relationship. Others saw us as just a perfect couple. At that point I didn't have enough life's wisdom to find a way to resolve this situation, and I wasn't bold enough to say the hell with everyone and leave. I wasn't bold enough to choose solitude in place of my calm, even, secure marital life. But I so wanted to!! And of course, if you can't manage something yourself, someone always turns up to help you. My helper took the form of a young, handsome, immeasurably sexy man whose clear mission was to drag me out of my cozy family nest into an abyss of passion, sex, total freedom and pleasure. Did he accomplish his mission? Yes and no. As a result of this infidelity, which was simply unavoidable in my case, I was forced to make a choice: my husband or my lover. And I had to do it at lightning fast speed, because every day I spent divided and undecided caused me unbearable torment. I had so wanted to find someone who would wrest me from the "paws" of my repellent husband. I had wanted love so much, I'd wanted to love and be loved. And that happened. I got everything I'd wanted. A stormy romance full of passion, the feeling that I was flying, happiness, sleepless night, and hundreds of secret text messages every night... But I couldn't handle it. I'd bitten off more than I could chew – and what I'd bitten off was so emotionally intense that I couldn't take it in. I choked. It turned out that I wasn't ready to leave my husband for the sake of delight and love. It's possible that I lacked courage, that I was cowardly. It's possible that that damned social opinion and my Christian worldview won out: people would exchange glances. What would they say and think - she left a husband who was so wonderful in all ways for a young green lover.   And what about the children? Would they understand? It turned out that everything resolved itself rather quickly. It seemed impossible to keep hiding the situation from my husband, but shocking him with the news of my infidelity seemed even less bearable.   And so I just ran away, like the gingerbread man in the fairy tale.   Ran away from everyone in the world. I made an unexpected decision – unexpected even to myself. To live alone!!!

Being a Spiritual Loser

The real tragedy of life is that we get old too early and wise too late.

So, I made the key decision to distance myself from everything love-related and from self-analysis and begin a new independent life. But that's not at all what happened! The film called "My Life" had its own screenplay that didn't figure at all in the director's imagination – at this point I considered myself nothing less than the director of my own life. It caught me totally by surprise when all of a sudden, for no visible reason, two of my organs stopped working. It's hard to believe something like this could happen, especially for a materialist, who considers matter one part of life and existence something entirely different. But someone who has even a superficial belief in the connection between cause and effect doesn't even need to be told what two organs they were. There's no need to spell it out. It's all perfectly clear. The most sensitive spot there can be in the female body – that's where I was struck, and that's what I lost. Both of my ovaries refused to function, menstruation fell off sharply, and all the doctors gave me the same disturbing diagnosis: early menopause. I should point out that before this, I'd never had any kind of problems in this department. At the time I'd just turned 33. The doctors were clear about it: early ovarian depletion and menopause. They say menopause is a disease of wisdom. All women experience it around age 50. Well, so what if I developed this "wisdom" early, at 33? But I didn't take much joy in this kind of wisdom. The only treatment for this diagnosis was – and still is – hormone replacement. One doctor after another painted me horrible pictures of how my organism would age prematurely. I could expect osteochondrosis, bruises over my entire body, insomnia, congestion, weight gain, irritability, psychosis and similar companions of old age – and all of this was dumped on me at 33! Most of the doctors were sincerely sorry for me, although this pity took a different form with each kind of doctor. The gynecologists said, "It's good you already had children. Don't tell your husband what's going on. Don't show him any test results."

How I got through this is its own special story. I call this period my spiritual loser period. Yes, I felt like a spiritual loser, because in spite of all the literature I'd read, and although I had some understanding of spiritual questions and had studied the law of cause and effect for many years, I still couldn't accept what had happened. I just wanted to die, to close my eyes and not wake up again. My life lost all meaning. Sure, I was in a better position than millions of others on our planet who are ill – better off than the ones who are paralyzed or crippled or terminally ill. I understood all that, but I still couldn't get a grip. Every day I functioned like a nocturnal animal. I'd take the kids to school and then go to bed. I'd sleep all day, because at night, I'd be suffocated by tears. I'd cry, I'd have nightmares, I'd experience all the horrors my doctors had said I would – I felt congested, tossing between hot and cold. It got to the point that my husband would come home from work at lunchtime just to fix the kids something to eat. I neglected my work and didn't answer the phone. Basically, I stopped getting out of bed. Antidepressants didn't help, although I took them by the packet. Then I became a big fan of sleeping pills, because taking them was the only way I could escape even a little bit. When I had to go to work, at least then I did have to pull myself together and get to the office, but I my behavior was even worse than when I stayed home. I'd down a glass of wine on an empty stomach, have some bitter chocolate, add in some strong coffee and get behind the wheel. There was just no other way I could do it. I hated myself for living this way. For crying. For losing my strength. For hating my life, for the unpleasantness of the situation, for my weakness. And most of all for not believing in God. But I couldn't do anything about the latter. Even my husband, a lifelong atheist, began trying to convince me: "You're just ungrateful. You don't value what God's given you. You gave birth to two marvelous kids before your ovaries went on strike, and you should be grateful for that. Lots of other people don't even have kids, and nonetheless, they manage to live, but you lose all reason and act like the most self-centered person in the world, as if someone had just taken your cookie away." And he was absolutely right. I understood all of that intellectually. But I couldn't get my feelings and emotions under control. My depression dragged on and I couldn't see any light at the end of the tunnel. Where's my faith gone, I'd ask myself. Really, what makes one a believer? Is it being convinced that not a single hair can fall from someone's head without it being God's will? In other words, that all that happens is solely according to His Will, and that we just have to bear it? We simply can't understand Divine will – we're no more than blind kittens, and all we need is humility. Well, and some free will and wisdom. Humility, will and wisdom – I've always felt I was doing fine in those departments. But that was a giant illusion. My serious sufferings revealed the true nature of my faith and shook the unstable foundation of my worldview.

We need humility if we're going to be able to meekly accept the things we can't change, and we need some free will so we can change the things we can change, and wisdom, well, that helps us tell one from the other and decide when things in life need changing and when we need to just accept what we've been given. And it's precisely the wisdom part that causes me so many problems.

The question of whether to make changes or not, to act or not, whether to lay responsibility for everything on God or to keep some of it myself – that's been my dilemma my whole life. And you can't solve that question without life's wisdom. But we gain wisdom by suffering, and no one wants to suffer. And so it's a kind of Catch-22: we need wisdom, but there's no suffering. Here's another way to put it: we like to eat fish, but we hate fishing.

And so it ended up that by age 33 I was totally screwed. I understand that I ended up there because of my diseased worldview, because of my wrong approach to life, to people, to men, and to myself. And to God. Saying I had a rotten character would be putting it mildly. Millions of people have a rotten character, but two of their organs don't suddenly refuse to function, and if they do, then it's probably not so dramatically – accompanied by suicidal thoughts, depression and not giving a damn about everyone around them. Although if I look at it in a sober way, it wasn't the case that I didn't give a damn about myself. The opposite, actually. I was so good at comforting my beloved self that my bitter tears would flow the whole night through. I felt sorry for myself, went over and over the details of my fate, compared myself to other people, and cried some more. Then things began to get even worse. My nervously religious mind told me: a woman's destiny is to bear children. Here I am crying and suffering just because I can't have any more children. What if God suddenly gets mad at me for behaving this way and takes away what he's given me? It won't be hard for you to guess where these thoughts led me. To utter panic and terror. I began hovering over the children. I turned into a mother hen, which is not at all in my nature. I began to be afraid of anything that might possibly threaten the children. In addition to my general depression, I began to be plagued by bad dreams. I lose the children. I see they're in danger, but I can't do anything about it. In general, I saw no way out of the situation. I knew that time heals. But would it heal me? Maybe it heals others. But my knowledge hindered me. I felt like packing up all the books that had filled up the apartment by this time and taking them out of the house, throwing them out. Like getting rid of all the self-help books about how to survive in this world, and all the spiritual literature, too. I wanted to clear my mind of all my accumulated garbage, and by age 33 I'd accumulated plenty of it. It was easy enough to give all my books away to my friends, but clearing out my brain...

Not taking into account all that you know, rejecting everything, that means returning to a purely materialistic mode of existence. But going back to that when you're only just beginning to move from theory to practice? That path leads straight to degradation. But that's not even the point. Having knowledge but acting as if you knew nothing and didn't want to know about anything, is to know the law and consciously violate it. If you live a purely ordinary life, without trying to understand or figure anything out, then you don't have to delve into things. But in my case there was no place to retreat to. I couldn't clear out the matrix, I couldn't erase anything from my memory, and I couldn't unlive my unpleasant experiences. That meant I had to learn to live with what I did have to work with. And on that particular day here's what I had: a horribly bad character, complete dissatisfaction with my life, no love for anyone, no matter who they were, most of all for myself, and then, menopause at 33, which resulted from my bad habit of using men, my huge sense of guilt, and various other stresses.

I couldn't leave things the way they were. I had to change something, myself first of all. Unfortunately, all my knowledge was theoretical in nature. I couldn't make practical use of it. The books of the great masters and teachers didn't help me. I soaked all of it up like a sponge, accepted it all and understood it, but I wasn't able to change myself. I was into books by Osho, Krishnamurti, Gurdjieff, Uspensky, Castaneda, and many others. I knew lots of things, but I didn't feel any better as a result. In theory everything was in place, but in practice... even meditation was so difficult for me that I simply gave it up. I ordered myself to change, got angry at myself because nothing was working, and blamed myself for everything that had happened. I nagged at myself every day, ate away at myself. I called myself a spiritual loser and wanted to burn all my books. I became firmly convinced that if a person's sick, that means they've brought in on themselves, that it's their own fault. I was living with a huge feeling of guilt. The only thought in my head was that I needed to change. But how? How can you change yourself, how can you move in any direction, when you're surrounded by darkness? On the other hand, if I'm an asshole, what can I expect to see around me? Darkness. I was already concerned not so much with a cure as with my future life. How was I to live from this point on? I can't be cured – you can't treat menopause. But somehow I had to live. And we have a choice: to be happy or to keep dragging out our miserable existence. In other words, to feel sorry for ourselves, to be overcome by the fear that something bad will happen, to be afraid of life, and to complain about the way things are.

After my next visit to the doctor, who yet again prescribed a bunch of hormone replacement drugs, I came to the decision that I'd go to a certain sage who, according to those with first hand experience, knew everything. There was lots of talk about this amazing person in our town: a sage who's the second Vanga, who can tell the future, reveal your life's mistakes to you, and so on. The hour long trip to the little village where the clairvoyant lived flew by. My head was full of questions about my health, about hormones and whether I should be taking them or not, about my personal life, about a great many things. This sage turned out to be a woman slightly older than I. She listened to my pulse while mulling over the information I gave her, and then she asked me sharply, "Why have you come to me? You don't need to do things like this. You know everything yourself. Put those pills in your hand, hold them there, and you'll be able to tell on your own whether you should be taking them or not. What happened to you, it happened when you were 33 because the time had come for it to happen. Now it's time to do some thinking. Soon you'll have a different level of consciousness and this kind of thing won't bother you, but for now you're so fearful, and that's hindering you. Don't be afraid. Oh, and also, you need to start writing a book. That's your destiny." Our conversation ended there. Everything I'd heard seemed like total nonsense. How can you not pay attention to the fact that you're not menstruating, to those nighttime energy surges and the insomnia? As far as a book was concerned, that seemed like a fantasy to me – never in my life had I written anything except a little article for our local newspaper. Once I got home I took a stab at figuring out whether I needed to take those hormones. I put the medicine in my hands, held it there, and felt nothing. I felt I had been duped. The next day I decided to go see her again. I needed her to tell me something specific about taking that medicine, and not some instruction to sense it myself. These are powerful hormonal substances, and they can have a whole series of side effects, including breast cancer. All the doctors were adamant that I needed to start taking them, and the sooner, the better. So I had no time for sensing. When she saw I'd come a second time, the wise woman started laughing. "Take the medicine. You don't know any other approach yet." It wasn't until several years after this that I realized what my illness was, and was able to understand and accept it, feel grateful that it had been sent to me, take myself off the hormones and begin the path to recovery. But these years of my life weren't easy.

Since my disease was strictly a women's disease, and since its causes lay in my relationships with men, that meant I needed to set things right in that department. Really, any type of gynecological illness always lies in a woman's faulty relationship to men. I went back again to my age-old question – am I able to be in love? Do I love? Am I loved? I couldn't figure all of this out without making changes in my life. So I decided to take a desperate step – I ran. I felt like running as far away as possible, where no one would know me, where I could be alone, figure myself out and start again with a clean slate.

It's possible that if I'd chosen my lover over my husband, I never would have gotten sick, wouldn't have left my country, wouldn't have written this book and would never have thought deeply about love. Perhaps I would simply have been living in love. Or, maybe the opposite would have happened. I could have turned into a philistine, concerned only with my appearance and whether I was too old to keep my young handsome husband. Or maybe I'd have had a baby and found a different meaning in life, in diapers and baby shirts. But that would have been an entirely different story and fate, the fate of a different woman on the path to her happiness. But the past doesn't belong to us. It's not ours. We're no longer its masters. It's already God's will, and our only task is to approach it in the right way.

A New Life

**Real meditation begins
when spiritual searching ends.**

And so I left home: an emotional wreck, directionless, disappointed, lacking any orientation in my life, aging and with a disturbing diagnosis that obviously confirmed the early setting of my moon, with two children and three suitcases. I left not just my home, but the country where I'd been born, and my favorite city, where I'd lived my whole life and where I had friends. I gave up an interesting, high-paying job. I left all my acquired possessions. But most important, I left my husband, and made him deeply unhappy. I left him alone with no way to see his children, with no possibility of having a family. My relatives and friends judged me harshly. And they all felt sorry for him! And they not only felt sorry for him. They raised him to the ranks of nobility. He gave me permission to take the children out of the country, saying he respected his wife's decision and couldn't hold her back by force. This was not at all the way an Eastern man would act and it was totally at odds with the traditions of our family and country. So I ended up being the bad gal in this story. Society saw only the tip of the iceberg. Our inner spiritual trials and searches for happiness were all beneath the surface, invisible to those around us.

Where did my path into myself begin?

With a primitive knowledge of English, two thousand dollars in my pocket, and without any idea of how I'd get by, I flew across the ocean and settled in Vancouver. You're out of your mind, my friends wrote, come back. You won't survive, my husband told me, you'll fall apart and come home. You're too spoiled by attention, by your social position. You had a career in your own country, social status. But there you're no one and nothing. And my husband was perfectly correct. In this foreign country I was an immigrant from a third world country with no means of existence. My education and work experience were worthless here, plus my English was bad. What could I do in a foreign country? But at that point I'd already stopped trying to prove anything to myself or anyone else. At that point I was no longer looking for a privileged life, or benefits. I wasn't torn by doubts, and I'd stopped living like some kind of isolated invalid who's always asking for something from life. Many would call this state depression, a lack of desire to life and achieve something. But I call this state the beginning of spiritual growth and an unbelievable leap forward on the path of coming to know myself. It was a leap from egoism to selflessness, to apprenticeship, to searching for love as a state of being rather than a sense experience.

Once I crossed the ocean I landed on another planet. Going from a small provincial city in a country many people haven't even heard of, I ended up in civilization, which is not what I'd been looking for. I hadn't been looking for new things, or material comfort, or good luck or recognition or freedom. I'd already had all that. I was looking for spiritual peace, for myself. India or Tibet would have been just as successful a choice for the move, but since my children were traveling with me, Canada looked safer. Had I been alone, I might have headed for India without a second thought. I wanted to live without doubts, without the distraction of my thoughts, I didn't want to feel disharmony within me. I really felt like going home, but not in the sense of having a roof over my head, but in the sense of having a home for my head. My mind needed to find a home. I was tired of wandering and roaming through the long senseless labyrinths of my mind. I was tired of being under the control of my ego, tired of the constant feeling of guilt, the constant feeling of superiority. Tired of being controlled by my head, which needed a home, I searched for one everywhere. For most people who start a spiritual search for the truth, that means always moving in the direction of something undefined, incomprehensible, something which exists but which we can't reach right now. I felt I was being led toward something, and to me that felt like the desire to find a home of my own and realize my potential, not just as a female, but also to achieve some kind of full completion, unity, peace and calm. Due to my given knowledge set, I couldn't blindly believe in a God sitting in the heavens and sending us gifts or non-gifts. At the same time, I sincerely envied people who accepted this model of the world. They weren't torn by doubts, they went to church on Saturdays without fail, they believed in the Heavenly Kingdom and made whatever efforts they could to reach it. I envied them, because they'd already found their God. I don't know whether they went further in their development, or whether you even need to do that. Live, do good, pray for the health of your family and those close to you, help people, and don't complicate your life. I liked that model of behavior a lot, but to my great misfortune, it was not a fit for me. In Canada, just as everywhere else I've been, by the way, I quickly found myself surrounded by a circle of people of various religions who in turn invited me first to one church and then to another. People with deep knowledge of the Bible, the Koran and the Vedas, masters of theosophy, seminarians. I had a close relationship with the pastor of a local Catholic church, was friends with the priest of an Orthodox church. I took a lot from Protestantism, liked Muslims and couldn't stand egotists. I liked these people of deep faith, all of them. Each had his own faith. Each had traveled his own path of spiritual searching and had found what he'd been looking for, gained peace, and come to believe. And I was constantly asking myself, why isn't this working for me? Why is my mind constantly asking questions, and why don't I like the answers the preachers give me? Why won't my mind calm down? Why do I always want to go "home"?

The First Step

**"If you're smart, you don't go up the mountain.
If you're smart, you go around it,"
said the ant as he looked at the train tracks.**

Once I settled in Canada, I came to the full realization that I hadn't escaped my problems. That all the same demons were still there in my head, that there were no fewer of them, that they hadn't gotten lost along the way or died, but had, in fact, actually increased. That's because a bunch of everyday problems got added to the spiritual problems: rent, getting the children settled in school, learning the language, looking for work. My husband had always taken care of all that. Here I had to bear the burden of all these unfinished tasks. And in addition to that there was fear, terrible fear. I was alone in this country. I had children for whom I was responsible. Children whose fate I'd decided in the space of an instant and whom I'd snatched out of their familiar surroundings. Did I have the right to do that? Around me were many countrymen from the former Soviet republics, emigres who'd been living here for decades. And almost all of them were dissatisfied with life in this foreign land. Almost all of them were unhappy. Even though some – a minority – were very successful. They had gotten an education here and begun careers and had a good income. But once I got to know them better, even they complained about how hard it was to live in a foreign country, about the nostalgia that hadn't faded over the decades, and about their desire to put everything back the way it had been. In spite of their success and their decades of living in this foreign country, these people keep on counting each year they'd lived and dividing their lives into "before" emigration and "after." After many heart to heart conversations with my countrymen and becoming a witness to a variety of fates (people are very open about sharing their experiences living in a strange land with newcomers,) I came to the conclusion that people really are unhappy, unliberated and crushed by life in a foreign land. As far I as was concerned, personally I saw nothing positive about my move. I didn't get rid of my demons, didn't get enlightened, developed a whole bunch of doubts, and along with the doubts arose new worries, my first gray hairs, and a short temper. Once again a wave of complaints about myself swept over me, guilt resurfaced, I was uncertain about whether I'd chosen the right path, and I was dissatisfied with myself. Overall, you could say that this old lady had wanted a new trough... and she'd gotten one.

Of course there definitely were positive aspects of the move. If a person is chock full of shit – by which in this case I mean that they possess "a mind that's lost its way," and this shit rules the ego and the head (which is full of the everyday familiar crap, nonsense and fetid air that make their way through the corridors of the mind) then there are only two ways to deal with it. The first is to empty out the pail of this shit all at once. True, it often happens that then our head immediately fills up again with fresh shit that doesn't stink only because it's new. The second approach is to stop filling it up, which will at the very least give you a short breather. I really don't know how you'd go about the first method in practice. It's probably more theoretical. We can't achieve enlightenment through force of will, just because we want to. We can't free our mind from its busyness, seal off that rushing stream – i.e., our mind – and, with a clean slate, begin a new life full of calm and harmony. All we can do is exchange one kind of shit for a different kind, and we can't even do that all at once. We do it gradually, and even then we can do it only if it's comfortable for our mind to do it, if it allows us to do it, in other words, if it sees a reasonable reason for doing so. Now the second method – not filling our minds with what's already there in abundance, that we can do. In this case we go through a kind of shift in our priorities. We don't part with what we've accumulated, and we don't try to get rid of it or forget it or live through it. We just pack it all up, archive it and store it on one of our shelves. We simply stop "poking around" in that area. The pail no longer keeps feeling up. It just sits there. In its own good time it will definitely start stinking and let us know it's there, but not right now. A packet of accumulated life's experiences can be compressed and dehydrated and not cause any more concern. In this case we say "time heals." Of course it can all come pouring out anew under certain external circumstances, and in that case we say, "the old wounds haven't healed." But in any case, whenever we strive not to fill up our pail any more, when we archive something, we always need to refocus our mind onto something new and unfamiliar. It's like when you're treating alcoholism with hypnosis – you need a replacement. It's the same with this. For example, someone who's never done physical labor can benefit from hauling bricks, while tradesmen can try working with canvas. Even so, none of this will bring any benefit or relief if we're more focused on receiving than on giving. For example, if you're in an abyss of troubles that have collapsed on top of you, then going out to the lobby of your apartment building and vacantly scrubbing the walls or the floors will help you more than any antidepressants. Why? Because you're just giving without expecting anything in return. But you do get something. If you're have a hard time emotionally and you go to a hospital and spend an hour caring for the patients, you'll feel better. It's the same law of giving at work. You give forth without thinking about exchange, you simply give, which means that in time you'll definitely get a return on your work in the form of a new dose of energy. That's how it all works. We give out energy and receive it in return. My emigration to Canada was like a test of this law of energy, and it helped me stop filling up the already overfilled garbage pail called my mind. Now I had to devote a lot of energy to things I didn't understand, to work I didn't believe in, to people I barely knew. I just blindly followed my daily routine, the routine I had to accomplish because there was no one but me to do it. I filled out various forms, studied English, got the kids to school, looked for work. In other words, I survived. That really helped me. It helped me put my thoughts in order. Or to put it more precisely, I just had no time to go rummaging around in myself. My everyday routine sucked up all my energy. All the doubts, worries and feelings of guilt that arose in my head when I got to Canada didn't grow any stronger and couldn't become powerful, because there was no time to feed them. My life forced me to do something, go somewhere, do this and that, deal with everyday problems. And it was great. Finally, for the first time in many years, I stopped thinking. Yes, paradoxical as it may seem, I stopped spending time on idiotic reflections on my life and feelings, stopped searching for the truth and instead started just living. Living a full life. Living like everyone else! Sure, a lot of people would probably call that surviving, not living. We saved money every way we could. I stopped wearing Armani and started shopping at Value Villages and thrift stores and didn't feel the slightest bit less happy because I was sifting through other people's used things. Sure the children whined. My older son often asked me, "Mom, why did we move here if we were going to live like beggars? At home we had everything." I couldn't answer that question. It would have taken too long to explain what had led me to emigrate. That I'd fallen out of love with his dad? Or that I'd been unable to solve my psychological problems? Or that I was searching for something? A 15-year old adolescent can't get that. Even I had a kind of difficult time sorting through the clump of feelings that had led me to decide on such a serious step. During our first months there, I studied the Canadian educational system and wrote and sent off articles about life in Canada to our local paper back home. But after a year the novelty of émigré life wore off. The new lifestyle that had intoxicated me in the first months was replaced by an awful fear for the future of my children. The honeymoon period was over. I was tired of going to school to study English, tired of smiling at people when I wasn't at all up to smiling. I began to doubt the sincerity of everyone around me. I didn't understand why people would ask, "How are you?" if they weren't really interested in the answer. But most of all I began to worry about my own survival. I began a more intensive work search, sending out 20-30 resumes every day, since it wasn't realistic to live on $8 an hour. But I didn't get any interviews out of it. I so wanted to go home. I was tired of surviving. I hadn't found any like-minded people – I was shy about interacting with Canadians because of my English, and I didn't have any interest in the circle of my fellow countrymen, since the only thing they ever talked about was how to survive in emigration and where to get money. On top of that, I began to worry about my younger son. He was absorbing his new culture and language so quickly that he was beginning to lose his native language, and I couldn't keep up with him in English. I saw that the longer he was here, the more he'd move away from me and forget his heritage. In our country there are some very deeply rooted traditions – children listen to their parents unconditionally and respect them deeply. I understood that things were different in Canada. A couple more years here, and he'd simply be unable to survive in the country where he'd been born. He couldn't read or write in his language, he'd grow up as a Canadian with a different way of thinking, not ours. All these thoughts more turned me more and more homeward, to my husband, who continued waiting and never stopped complaining that he'd lost the chance to raise his children. My thoughts tended more and more in the direction of "you have to go back now, before it's too late." It would be better for everyone. We need to live where we're born. This country will never be my native land. Why make the effort, if I can go back to where everything is ready and waiting and live a happy life? In the midst of all of this – my doubts and uncertainty and my inability to make the right decision, my not knowing how to live from now on – shocking news arrived from home.

The World Turns Upside Down

Early morning, and I'm awakened by a phone call from home. It's eight in the morning. My brother's on the line, his voice alarmed: "Something terrible has happened. Vyacheslav has died." Vyacheslav is my older brother. He was young, healthy, successful and stable. He lived his whole life with our mother, was the sole support of the household, helped my other brother, and me, too, sometimes. The circumstances were tragic – he fell asleep in the car. It took them a long time to work up to calling us. My husband refused to be the bearer of such news. My mother was in shock from what had happened. So it fell to my younger brother to break the news. At the moment when I grasped what had happened, I just cried out. From helplessness, pain, and from lack of understanding about why it had happened this way. Why now, why him. If the news had been about my younger brother, maybe I would have taken it more easily. A man who abused alcohol, led an irregular life, had no purpose, work or family. But the one who died was happy, and not a drinker, someone who lived correctly in all ways. I couldn't explain what had happened. My mind deserted me. I don't know what was going on with me at that moment. Within the first hour, I bought tickets on the next flight and found someone to take care of the kids. But an hour later I returned the tickets and decided not to go anywhere. I didn't have the strength to make the trip. Or maybe I simply didn't want to see him dead, to face and accept this. But the next day I looked for tickets again, and when I'd bought them, I realized I wouldn't get there in time for the funeral. My mind, in a state of shock, rushed about like a beast caught in a trap. I ended up not going to the funeral. Probably out of faintheartedness. Even though it was more complicated to go through the grief alone. Perhaps if I'd ended up being there then with my family, I would have had an easier time of it. I couldn't have a really good cry in front of the children – I didn't want to upset them even more. They'd lost their favorite uncle, they'd been the meaning for his entire life. On the day of the funeral I berated myself for not being there, not being with my mother. Really, what was I doing here? There was one answer to this – experiencing losses. My mother had told me that my brother had a very hard time being apart from his nephews and couldn't wait for summer vacation, that he'd already begun stocking up on gifts for the little boys. He had no children, so my sons were the recipients of all his unrealized paternal love. He called them in Canada every day. He died in March. He didn't make it the three months left until summer vacation. We saw him before we left for Vancouver, and that ended up being the last time we saw him. Who knew then that we'd never see each other again... Now thoughts about what would happen to my mother tormented me. She'd lived her whole life with my brother, but now he was gone, I was gone, and her grandsons, too. We couldn't place any hope on our brother – a hopeless alcoholic. I felt drawn back home. I decided to wait until the school year ended and then go back. Staying in Canada was unbearable. I didn't know how to fill those three months until the end of the year, how to occupy myself. At that moment I felt like a robot. Running on autopilot, I did the work around the house, cooked for the children, hardly ate anything myself, and lost a lot of weight. Everything got done only because it had to. One day, because I couldn't bear all of this insanity, I signed up for a meditation group run by Mada Dalian. Her book about the Path had garnered great interest among readers and won several awards. It turned out the author lived in Vancouver. And it also turned out that Dalian's meditation program, based on Osho's system, was not the cheapest way to go. But the price didn't stop me. I took all the money I had left and used it to pay for the intensive ten-day meditation program.

The Beginning of the Cleanse
Day One

Trying to stabilize and extend the meditative state is like prolonging the pleasure of pissing in the bathroom.

Six in the morning. I'm nervous and can't go into the meditation hall. Mada senses my terror and comes out into the hallway. She gives me a hug. "Welcome. How did you find your way here?" There's such simplicity and sincerity in her words. I get even more nervous and mumble the traditional "Good morning." I had imagined this meeting many ways, but not at all this way. I make my way into the hall. Adepts, people searching for the truth, about ten of them, are sitting on the floor in a circle. I'm uncomfortable – everyone's speaking English. I'm terribly afraid of missing something, of not getting something important. They're talking about deep things, after all. A cameraman is filming Mada. All of a sudden she turns to me and asks, "Are you understanding us? If you want to ask something, ask me in your language. That's how you and I will work together." I felt a little better. So, she knows my language. I recall that in her biography it said that she was from one of the former Soviet republics. I'm sitting close to Mada and I just feel like throwing up. We're talking about our fears. Most people's are similar. Going around in a circle, each person is supposed to give voice to what he fears most in life. At first glance, this doesn't seem hard at all. But if you haven't done group work before, it's not an easy task. I sensed two main fears – fear for my children, the terrible fear of losing them, and the fear of being to blame, especially

57

for their deaths. There, I said it. Mada's commentary: good, now we know what to work on.

Mada gives us final instructions and asks for volunteers who've already done an intensive to show the newcomers what to do. The meditation begins. I have no right to describe what went on in detail. It was a private group. I couldn't wait for it to be over. I became nauseated from the breathing and could barely stay on my feet because I was so worn out. And it terrified me to think that I still had nine more days of this insult ahead of me, but it seemed a shame to leave – I'd already paid. By nine in the morning I made it back home, barely alive. And I felt even worse just from thinking about the fact that the next day I'd have to get up again at 4 a.m., drag myself to a different city and put up with all this confusion yet again.

Toward evening I checked my email and found ten Facebook messages. It turns out our group had a Facebook page. It wasn't open to other internet users. Mada would put "homework" up on it: each of us was supposed to share the experiences we'd had overcoming patterns during meditation, and read others' accounts of their efforts. A kind of collective work. Only my message, the 11th one, was missing. But for some reason I wasn't up to doing my homework.

Day Two

It's Saturday, and I have no idea how I'll get to where meditation is held. Mada always starts right at six in the morning, not a single minute later. My neighbor helps me out and gives me her car for Saturday and Sunday.

Mada goes around in a circle, telling each person what his inner problems are and what he should work on during meditation. She gets to me. "You're afraid of not pleasing others." I object. "I don't think so. I always do what I want and don't worry much about others." She adds, "Of course you don't think so, because this is going on unconsciously, it's an old pattern, from a past life. You're stuck in it and should get rid of it. Repeat in your native language, 'My life won't fall apart if I stop doing what others want me to do.'" She says all of this in English, but I'm blocked. I can't repeat all of that in my native language. Or don't want to. I repeat her words mechanically in English, that's easier for me. I never thought it would be easier for me to say something in a foreign language, than in my own. But Mada won't leave me in peace. She keeps insisting I say it again, loudly, but in my own language. I admit my weakness. She starts me off. She says the first word in the sentence for me, and I carry on from there. She asks me to do the same thing several times, loudly. I do it. The others listen. I'm embarrassed. Mada's response: oyoooi. My conclusion: we're off! During meditation I feel much better. Not at all tired. I even found some moments interesting. After meditation our little brotherhood shares its thoughts: "Each time things will get more and more interesting, amazing things will start happening, and the main thing is to notice them. It's especially important not to miss meditation on the day when you have no desire at all to drag yourself here, because that's usually the day something happens." Okay, that cheers me up. Especially the thought that I'm not the only one who doesn't feel like dragging themselves here.

I returned home in a more elevated mood than on the first day.

Day Three

We're sitting on the floor in a circle. Instead of doing our traditional discussion, Mada suggests we work with our breath. Each one of us has to stand up and breathe in a certain way. And she watches the energy as we do so. Where's there a block? How far up is the energy able to rise? She explains that we put the blocks there ourselves, and that we can remove them ourselves, too. She tells each person about his blocks, about the problems his mind has created. Almost everyone begins crying as they carry out these instructions, during this execution. Her words bring us all to tears, because they sting us to the quick. She doesn't spare us. She doesn't soften the blow with any of us, she says what she sees and makes us work. You can't hide anything from her. She forces us to look truth in the eyes. And since this isn't an individual session, but group work, each of us witnesses what happens. "You think this is your secret, and you keep it to yourself. But someone else has the same secret, and he keeps it to himself and thinks it's his secret alone. No, everyone has the very same secrets, so let them come out, don't hold them in." I wait my turn in terror. Most everyone else is done now. I'm up. I go into the center of the circle and begin breathing. After several minutes, Mada shouts, "Stop!" That means she's gathered her information and is ready to issue a verdict. Suddenly she asks me, "Do you know belly dancing? Can you do that for us?" "I'll try." "Then dance and keep on breathing." I dance. She shouts into a microphone: "Your hips, use your hips more, and your stomach, faster." Because of the specific nature of the breathing and the dancing I begin spinning around and end up turned 180 degrees, with my back to the group, but without being able to say how it happened. "Stop!" Mada shouts. "What do you feel? Where's your breath gone?" I feel heat throughout my whole body. "Very good. During meditation, keep on doing this, and don't worry if you end up at the other end of the hall without knowing how you got there. You've been frozen for many years. Why don't you take enjoyment in life? Take delight in your life, dance. And now tell everyone that you'll enjoy life, and that if anyone tells you that's wrong, you'll tell them to go to hell." I repeat that and take my seat. Today during catharsis time I'll work on this. Another member of the group takes my place.

I look around at the people in the group. I've known them for only two days, by I feel an inexplicable peace. I don't usually feel comfortable among English speakers, since I often don't get everything, especially jokes. But here, among these people I barely knew, I felt more comfortable than I've ever felt, even among my closest friends. Each of them was his own person. These people felt very close to me, close in spirit. They were of differing social status and age, but we were all sailing in the very same boat, all searching for the shore. I can put it another way: we're all united by our dirty laundry. We know it's dirty, but we keep on wearing it, and it so happened that today we were given a marvelous opportunity to wash it, all together. We took off everything and, weeping, we washed. And Mada served as the laundry soap. A very powerful cleaning agent, which she'd tested on herself. Her comments: "You've had a good cry, you've felt sorry for yourselves, and now let's get to work. Each of you knows what to do. Free yourselves of your blocks, they suck your energy. Don't be vampires sucking up someone else's energy." I danced a lot and asked Jessica (Mada's assistant) to note down for me what music Mada had put on when I was dancing.

Once again I was having trouble getting to my destination on time. I asked one of the girls in the group to pick me up at the station, all week, until Saturday. Her job was to work on the pattern of "knowing how to say no to people." That's why I didn't have a moment's hesitation about asking her to do me this favor: I knew that if it wasn't on her way, she wouldn't be shy about telling me. After all, I was among "friends" now.

Day Four

We began class with questions and answers. The students ask Mada about what's most urgent for them. I have a whole list of questions prepared, most of them general in nature, about world order, about life. I timidly ask Mada whether I can send her my questions by email. "I won't answer general questions, it's a waste of time. I'm prepared to answer questions related to you personally, your development, and I'll do that here, in the group, since it can benefit the others." So I had to set aside the general and shift to the private: "Well, for example, I've always been afraid of doing something wrong in my life, ruining my karma and committing a sin. What's right and what's wrong?" Mada: "Your main problem is Christianity. It's a burden to you. I know what Christianity means in the Soviet Union. I'm from there myself. Don't listen to the Bible, listen to yourself, open yourself up. Today during meditation breathe in earnest and don't be afraid. It's only breathing, not a sin." The group laughs and so do I. "How can I understand whether I love my husband?" Mada: "If you're asking yourself this question, it means something somewhere is missing, you've lost something. But you won't find the answer until you begin to trust yourself. What can you give to someone else, if you have nothing yourself, not even love for yourself?" "But self-love develops egoism, and I'm egotistical enough as it is." "What develops egoism is a strong lack of love for yourself. When we're not in a state of love, we demand others' attention and we need others' energy. That's what egoism is. But when we love, we don't need anything from others and we ourselves can give."

Today we did a new type of meditation. We used Osho's methods. We had to say "no" to everything, for a long time, and then say "yes", also to everything, and for a long time. Mada suggests we get into a comfortable position and she'll put on some music. I position my rear on a soft cushion and begin saying "no, no, no...." After a bit I hear Mada's voice near me: "Get up, shout 'no' loudly in your native language. Not mechanically. Feel your 'no'. Listen to your body, do what it tells you to do, and observe yourself while you do it." Within a few minutes I'm totally stomping my feet, waving my arms and shouting "no, no, no" in despair. It's interesting that I'm stomping mainly with my left leg and waving with my left hand, probably because I'm left-handed. A categorical "no" gives way to a playful "no", then to a doubtful "no", and so on and so forth. I hear my various "no's." This exercise goes on a very long time, and at this moment something really does happen with my consciousness. Then there's stark quiet, the music breaks off, and we're "hanging" in total quiet, also for a very long time. The music starts again, and we do the same thing with "yes." Personally, I liked my "yes" more. It didn't seem as aggressive, rather softer and more pleasant. Mada's comments: Good work today. Good for you. Our homework was to say "yes" to the things we usually say "no" to, and vice versa. To listen to ourselves. "If you always say 'yes', and you sense protest inside, then say 'no'. It's time to finally take responsibility for your lives." I'll do it. My first thought: should I say to my kids, I don't have any reading to do today, let's go out for pizza. My second thought: "to hell with pizza, it's Orthodox Lent, let the kids read instead." No, I'm a hopeless F-student.

Day Five

Our usual morning discussion. We're talking about hereditary patterns. "You'll keep repeating your parents' patterns until you wake yourself up from them. Observe yourself. Don't do anything mechanically. Life is a game, so just play it, but don't get caught up in it, be vigilant observers of all that happens in your life. Why worry about what might happen or what might never happen. We can't change the future, but we can begin to change the present. Start living."

Before meditation Mada asks me, "Natasha, why do you partly cover one of your ears during meditation, is it because of the loud music?" I answer that it gets congested from the breathing. "Work your arms harder, and that will stop." Why did Mada call me Natasha? She's fully aware that I have a different name. She's called me by name more than one, and I filled out the registration form and my check. How did I become Natasha today? I observe myself – I don't like that she called me by a different name. I get it that she just mixed my name up with another. But the thought's flying around in my head: "she's not at all enlightened." Can an enlightened bring forget something or get mixed up? I keep observing myself – how quickly my ego reacted to the slightest danger of losing its identity. Really, when you come down to it, what difference does it make to me whether she'd enlightened or not? Each of us answers for our own life: she for hers and I for mine. No enlightened person can give you what they have. So let her call me a potty if she wants. What's my ego's problem? It's so attached to every little thing. I just shut it down and begin meditating. Breathing, catharsis, standing in silence, and dancing. Each stage usually takes physical effort, and a lot of it. The more out of synch you are with your brain, the more physical effort it takes. When you can't "tune out," you have trouble with the extended jumping and standing still. You just can't wait for the end of the exercises. But when you're peaceful, then you have no body, you just don't feel it. For the first time today I understood how that works on a practical level. I stood without moving a muscle, not falling from one foot to the other, the way I usually do, to shift my weight. I just didn't feel my body. I don't know how long I might have been able to stand like that. But unfortunately, then my thoughts started racing around, like cockroaches. I wasn't able to get back into that state before meditation ended. I can't wait for tomorrow. Our homework is to count the benefits we gain from consciousness and the benefits of being in a state of sleep.

Day Six

One of my friends drops me an email. She asks me to ask Mada a question that's been bothering her. There's a problem when you realize that I am not a feeling. Accepting that "I am not the mind" is much easier. But what to do about feelings? How to get yourself heading in a new direction on that one? I promise to ask.

Morning discussion. Mada divides us into pairs and suggests we ask each other two questions. Our feelings and our thoughts: what are feelings, who feels them, and what are thoughts and who thinks them? She asks us not to look for an answer with our mind. She suggests we follow our breath and get a good feel for it. People came up with the most varied answers. The same answer came to me for both questions – the head. That's the place where I think and the place where I feel. Mada asks, "But who in the head thinks? Who feels?" The answer comes through another student. It's my unconscious.

Mada explains: "Don't confuse feelings with emotions."

Emotions are our habits, in the same category as the habit of drinking coffee in the morning, or smoking. Emotions are the habits we form over the years. We can't fight them, we have to observe them. They're only emotions, they aren't us. Feelings are the shoots of our conscious mind and they develop along with intuition.

During the Kundalini meditation nothing unusual happened, if you don't count that I closed my eyes in one part of the hall and opened them in another. I can't understand how it happened, because the whole time I was keeping observing my body with a single-pointed focus. How could I not have seen it move? I think something happens when you're breathing, and that at some point you go into "tuned out" mode.

On my way home I suddenly got a chill standing at the bus stop. I remember Mada's words: "Don't hold back. Enjoy life, play with life." I remember the jumping we did during meditation, and how warm I'd gotten doing that. I begin jumping. People are looking at me. But I don't care, I want to warm up. An old lady with a black bandage over one eye comes up to me. I recall that Kutuzov wore a bandage just like that. "Are you dancing?" the granny asks. I immediately begin justifying my actions. "It's cold, I was trying to warm up." And then the "Kutuzov" lets loose in a dance. I don't think she would have minded jumping a little, but her age wouldn't permit it. I stop jumping and begin dancing with her. The people around us are smiling. It's eight in the morning. We're dancing at a bus stop like two crazy people. Yes, this could probably happen only in Vancouver. A few more meditations with Mada and I'll be ripe for the loony bin, from "society's viewpoint."

I find lots of Facebook announcements. The group's actively discussing who it is in us that thinks and who is it that feels. But I don't feel at all like getting into that. At least not today.

Day Seven

There was a powerful storm in Vancouver overnight. Mada begins our discussion by talking about safety. The survival instinct arises from the collective unconscious, it's in our nature to be frightened, and we seek a place of safety. She asked what we'd felt during the storm. It had been nighttime, and the majority of us had been sleeping. "You're unconscious, that's why you were sleeping. In this storm I sensed the approach of what's facing us in 2012. It will happen on December 21st, or maybe the 25th, but it will be quite unexpected. And afterwards, those who survive will begin to change, a transformation of consciousness will occur. They'll build a new world. We need to accept everything that comes. Meditate, be calm, be a witness of what happens. We can't change anything." The group asks for advice about how to prepare for that day. Mada answers, "Begin spending your money. Forget about your bank accounts."

We did a new type of meditation to open our chakras. We breathed in a specific way. Before meditation we all got our rugs, cushions and blankets ready. I could barely manage to keep standing until the end of the meditation. My whole body ached, and a lot of saliva had collected in my mouth from having to keep my mouth open the whole time. We were allowed to sit down, but it was preferable to breathe while standing. Once we got the signal "Relax" everyone plunked down onto their waiting spots. I covered myself up from head to toe and crashed. I came to when the wake up signal sounded.

Mara's commentary: meditation went well, good for you. Homework: Think about what makes us slow down. Finish everything you do today. When we put something off to later, that saps our energy, it makes it hard for us to be in the "here and now." It was only when I left the meditation hall that I understood how well meditation had gone. There really was a feeling of a lot of energy. I want to do that again. My fellow students discussed it: yes, this was one of the best practices we've done.

Day Eight

One of the girls from the group has continued to pick me up at the metro station punctually at 5:30 a.m. But because of the bus I get to the station late today, so it ends up that we're both late to meditation. I decided to ride my bike to the bus. There aren't many cars on the road, I can get up a good head of steam and make it to the first train to downtown. I lock my bike up at the metro, and on the way home I lug it onto the bus.

Our traditional morning discussion. We're talking about sin. "Any religion is hypnosis. People go to church every Sunday to get even more hypnotized. You're not sinful, no one's going to punish you for your sins. Why does every religion say that sex is bad, that it's sinful? Because it's easier to control you that way. If you wake up and become conscious, it won't be possible to manipulate you, and so, religion isn't interested in having you wake up. If you say, I want to rejoice in my life, enjoy myself, I'm not afraid of anything, then what will they say to you in church? The church doesn't need people like that. The true religion is Zen. It's the religion of reality. It teaches you to know yourself. Learn to trust only what you've experienced, what you've gone through yourself. Don't believe anyone except yourself, everything else is hypnosis." I ask about karma. "How should I approach that, after all, karma functions, it's not hypnosis." "Yes, it functions, but only until your awakening. Karma doesn't punish you, it only shows you the mistakes you've made in your state of unconsciousness. It 'wakes you up,' forces you to go through all of it over and over until you change your ways. There's nothing bad about this, it's not punishment, you're punishing yourself."

I didn't do a good job during meditation. I was distracted by my damn apartment keys. When I left the house I couldn't find them anywhere. So I had to leave the door unlocked, and the children were asleep. Now I was distracted by two thoughts: the children's safety and, how, in the midst of practicing conscious awareness, could I have lost my keys? A girl in the group said, this is a perfect opportunity for you to "votch your mind" today. But "votch" it or not, I wasn't able to calm down and focus on my task. The burden on my mind lifted only after I called home to check on things. The kids were fine. It turned out my son had taken the keys and not put them back where they belonged. So, this time the lack of awareness wasn't mine.

Our homework: to do something today that isn't usually in our nature, something we never do. I spent the whole day sprawled out on the couch, which is precisely what I do every single day. I'm telling you, I'm an F student.

Day Nine

"Living without risk is a waste of time. Don't be afraid to take risks, take risks every day, live your life fully," Mada exhorts us. "More spontaneity in life. Don't be afraid of anything." Today we're doing a new meditation – mandala. This is an extreme meditation, but it's worth it. It's through this very type of meditation that many achieve their first experience of stillness, experience being outside their minds. We did this meditation at the request of one of Mada's students. By using very meditation he'd been able to go beyond the boundaries of his mind for the first time. Our task was to torment our body, squeeze everything out of it, wear ourselves out entirely and observe our mind. Before the meditation began, Mada suggested we pick a focal point, a spot in the room or outside the window, and look at it intently. We had to run in place while raising our knees high and all the while look at the object we'd chosen. We had to run for a very long time, until we couldn't run any more. At some point I felt like giving up this "aerobics", I really just had no more strength. All the while Mada kept saying: don't listen to your mind, your body can do anything, you are not your mind. And that helped a lot. When you force your mind to shut up, you get your second wind. When the "stop" signal sounds, you sit down on the floor and slowly rotate your head clockwise. Then you lie down and do the same thing. And while you're doing this, you take care to keep your gaze from wandering, and keep your eyes going around in a circle the whole time. In this case your eyes are an indicator of your mind – as soon as your mind goes where it's not supposed to, the eyes lose the given orientation. After rotating our eyes came the long-awaited relaxation. But even now we weren't released from the task of observing our mind. I don't know how the others felt about it, but I didn't like this way of meditating. Afterwards I went up to the student on whose request we'd tortured ourselves so much. I was terribly eager to ask him whether he'd managed to catch a piece of nirvana this time. "Unfortunately, this time nothing happened. It happened only one time, when my witness was much weaker than it is now. I regard it as a gift from above, things were opened up for me a little, I was shown that it's possible, so I'd keep working. It lasted for seconds." I had the thought that he'd escaped his mind that time precisely because of the weak witness. When your inner witness is stronger, maybe it doesn't allow that. But then why do we develop it? So that we can direct the mind, instead of being directed by it. I recalled that in her book, Mada had written that if you don't train both your lower center and the witness, then it can happen that you can't get back, from there.... (Yes ... if my mom reads this, she'll think I really have gone out of my mind.)

Exhausted, I dragged myself home. Tomorrow was the last day of meditation, and I was looking forward to it with mixed feelings. I felt sorry to take leave of the group, and I still had a bunch of questions for Mada, I felt these ten days weren't enough for me. Before beginning this ten-day intensive, I'd prepared a whole list of questions for Mada. Each day I'd cross out the ones I managed to ask during our morning discussion. I sent the rest to her by e-mail. I got the answer back that it was better to ask these questions during her regular live radio show appearances, so that more people could hear them.

Day Ten

Mada asks everyone who really does want to wake up to raise their hands. Everyone raises them. "Think about the source of this desire. If you really want that, then during today's meditation breathe as if you were taking your last breath. If you have doubts about whether you really need this, if you're content with your life, your suffering, then make a decision not to change anything and respect that decision." We begin the breathing. I truly want to awaken. I'm sick of sitting in a dungeon, sick of wandering through my mind's mazes. To do this I need to release all my earthly attachments, including the desire to live. I have to be ready to meet death. I spend a long time getting myself set. Damn it, I mean, I don't want to die. I understand that it's just my mind that grasps onto the earthly, my mind that's terrified of losing power. Finally I settle in and take a breath as if it were my last, fully accepting all that might happen at this moment. And suddenly the thought hits me: today is exactly 40 days since the day my brother died. Where is his soul now, has it already risen? I don't want to meet it. I grow horribly afraid. The ending signal sounds. Disappointed, I pack up my cushion. Mada brings us all together for a ceremony to mark the completion of the intensive. She presents each of us with a rose and gives individual instructions. She gets to me. It's my first intensive, so she asks me to share my experience. I say that I'm terribly disappointed. Nothing happened with my mind, I'm totally the same as I was, I haven't changed a bit. "Actually, you got a good start, people spend a lot of time understanding what they need to do with their mind and their thoughts. You made a good start. But don't try to conquer your mind. You need it, and you don't want to turn into a vegetable. All you need to do is observe it impartially, develop your inner witness. Work on that."

After receiving our instructions, we began to take some photos and dance. Then the whole group went out to breakfast at Café Zen. I was watching Mada the whole time. She's so calm and even. Always. I had the sense that she knows exactly what's going to happen in the next minute. But in actual fact, she doesn't know this, she just accepts everything, no matter what happens. Because of her complete acceptance, she has no terror, no worries, no desires. She's open to what is. That's why you get the impression that she knows and sees everything. But really, she's an ordinary person, like each one of us, except that she's come to know herself more deeply than any of us.

The Fruits of Meditation

And so, my ten days of meditation are behind me. I've spent not a small sum of money (at least by my standards) and quite a bit of energy. It's time to move from snot and feelings to action. As a practical person, I weigh the benefits. What did this intensive give me? I didn't receive enlightenment. I'm not experiencing total happiness. I let loose at the kids just as I used to, grumble about minor things and keep searching for something. But I keep practicing, looking for the "inner witness within me," just as Mada taught me to do. And this is precisely where a problem came up for me. This turned out to be pretty boring work. It's so much more fun to fly in the clouds – to spend time in the past or to shift myself into the future. But keeping my mind in the present gives me little pleasure. It's really boring for me to do that. On the radio show "Transformation," Mada answered my question about the boredom of being "in the now." It turns out that boredom is characteristic of beginners' practice. That's how the mind tries to lead us away from reality. However, reality really is precisely here and now. In moving us into the past or the future, the mind brings us only suffering.

I continue to practice my inner witness. It's gotten less boring than it was when I started out. If I manage to dive deeper into the meditative state, while watching my mind, then it even gets interesting. In essence, through meditation you can attain what drug addicts attain with the help of a dose of narcotics. Only these are called spiritual experiences. They definitely don't lead to enlightenment or to an understanding of the way things exist. They are simply experienced moments, simply experience, no different from any other in life. But spiritual experiences and practices of this kind are no joke, they can be a bit dangerous. For example, after completing a strict forty-day fast, I allowed myself to have some wine for Easter. Once back at home, I sat down to do my evening meditation. And you'll never guess what began to happen with my inner witness... Evidently "it" was drunk. The mind began hallucinating. I couldn't stop the hallucinations, not even by opening my eyes. I understood that alcohol and conscious awareness don't mix. If you're going to drink, then drink and enjoy the "freedom" alcohol gives you. But if you're a meditator, then enjoy the freedom that vigilance gives you.

The ten-day intensive introduced me to the world of meditation. I'm grateful to Mada for that. I've taken my first steps in that direction. Now I fly in the clouds a lot less. I'm here and now more often. I've begun to see myself, my strong points, and my inadequacies. That is so great! Now I get pleasure not from reading something or spending time with someone, but just because I "am." I just am. It's gotten amazingly interesting for me to be with myself. I walk along the street and enjoy that. The period of being bored when my mind was "here and now" has been replaced by the pleasure of seeing myself and all around me. I've begun to see the sky, birds, the sun, people, and my own mind. Just now it led me back to a conversation I had yesterday with a friend, and a minute later it moved me to the problem of some tickets I haven't bought yet. Now I'm able to totally keep up with my mind, and it couldn't be any other way, because now I keep an eye on all the "cockroaches" in my mind, they no longer multiply at the speed of light. I can "exterminate" them. My mind no longer rules me the way it did before. I no longer fight with it, but just watch it. I don't know why I do this or whether I need to do it, but I can't do things any other way. I know it's impossible to keep an eye on all my thoughts – I often discover that my inner witness disappears somewhere, and my mind loads me up with problems of its own making. But when I "come to," I don't get at all mad at myself, I laugh at myself, thinking, how did I fall asleep again? Yet another moment of life passed me by, while my mind was wandering in the past or the future. But really, the majority of us generally live only in the past or the future, without knowing the present at all. Isn't that horrible?

After the intensive I also stopped fearing for my life so much. I became less attached to my body and to some earthly things. I pretty much don't think about my illness any more. I've fasted for 56 days with ease. I've been doing that for many years, each spring. But this year in particular I barely noticed any hunger at all. It was the easiest fast of my life. Even so, I sill get caught up in fearing for my children's lives. I don't know whether I'll ever free myself of that attachment, from the false perception that "they're mine," from the desire to "keep them safe," from being afraid for them. I keep working on that, although for me, the children remain the most complex sphere of liberation from earthly attachments.

But the main thing I've begun noticing and feeling is that the very stuff I'm made of is somehow new. It's kind of hard to describe. I just feel that I'm different. I don't know why I feel that way. Whether it's because of the circumstances I've lived through, or from my attempts to practice conscious awareness, but it's as if the scales have begun to fall off of me a little bit each day. And new scales grow in their place. This process is very precious to me and I don't want it to stop. For now I still have a great deal of old skin, and I want more change, I want all the old to come off me. And I don't fear the new. I like myself, I like the renewed me. Perhaps this is just temporary euphoria, and maybe after a while I'll spring back to my former state? Although something tells me there's no way back. On the level of everyday life in society, I'm still a complete asshole – with no husband, no work, no money – but all the same I'm no longer looking for a measured and secure future with a familiar stability. That is so boring. Yes, I'm ambitious, I love comfort and expensive things. But the ambitions of the material world are no longer capable of taking possession of me more than the desire to know myself, to find truth. I stuff myself full with reading the enlightened beings of all times and lands. In recent decades a lot of people have been writing about enlightenment from the viewpoint of their own personal experience. They call themselves enlightened. How lucky they are! But I have the feeling that these contemporary enlightened folks will soon start competing to see whose enlightenment is higher. You can't always tell from reading their books who's enlightened and who's not. A person might refer to any spiritual experience or personal transformation as enlightenment. But suffering students, wanting to become enlightened, you can always find those everywhere. If only there were a teacher. Although of course, enlightenment is… wait a minute… at this point I'd better turn to what's been published on this topic by the enlightened ones and by those who consider themselves among their ranks.

Sri Aurobindo Ghose (India)
I was thrown into such a state above thought and without thought, which was not obscured by any mental or vital movements whatsoever; there was neither the

ego nor the real world –– only, as I looked through static feelings, something sensed or connected the world of empty images, materialized shadows, lacking in any real substance, to its own absolute silence. This was neither a mental realization nor a fleeting illumination shining from somewhere on high –– it was not an abstraction –– it was positive, the sole positive reality which, although it was not the spatial physical world, filled up this appearance of the physical world by means of itself, occupied, or rather, flooded and submerged it, leaving no space for any other reality except itself, and allowing no one, except itself, to appear real, positive of substantial... It (this experience) brought the inexpressible Peace, amazing silence, and the unboundedness of liberation and freedom.

Wayne Liquorman (USA)
It was a quantum difference, not one of "unity." The whole status of things, the very center of things, changed. My point of view is that before you reach complete understanding and realization, you experience being present. After that, the person who would experience being present no longer exists. You can only experience that from which you're separate. For that reason, the experience of being present no longer means anything, because there's no duality. There's only presence.

Ramesh Balsekar (India)
But this thing that happened inside appeared in the form of a full and complete change. The only external change I could detect was an unusual feeling that my body was weightless. I couldn't put a name to it, and that state continued on for another day or two before settling down. That's how it happened. As I've already said, it was a peaceful occurrence, unexpected, of

78

course, very unexpected... absolutely spontaneous. The understanding arose that there is no such thing as an individual who would want this or that. The state already exists here. The absence of the "I" who would want anything to happen – that's the final state before this can occur.

Osho Rajneesh (India)

The universe is waiting. It sees that you're working on yourself, and all that time it doesn't butt in, it just waits. It can wait an infinitely long time, because it doesn't suffer from the need to act. It's Eternity itself. But at the very moment when you leave your efforts behind and disappear, the entire Universe rushes to meet you and fills you up. That's the precise moment when everything begins.

My state was supernatural. The first time, it shakes you to the very depths of the soul. After that experience you can never again go back to being the way you were before. It brings with it entirely new views on life and makes you totally different.

Around midnight my eyes suddenly opened, all on their own... in any case, I didn't make any effort to do this. Something had disturbed my sleep. Next to me, in my room, I sensed someone's presence. My room was totally tiny, but everywhere around me I felt the beating of life, powerful vibrations. It was as if I'd fallen into the eye of a typhoon and was being swallowed up in a majestic storm of light, joy and blessedness.

It was so real that everything else grew unreal: the walls of my room, the entire house, my very body. Everything grew unreal, because only now had I seen genuine reality for the first time.

That's why it's difficult for us to understand when Buddha and Shankara say that the world is Maya, an illusion. We know only this world, our world, and we have nothing with which to compare it. We know only one reality. What are these people talking about? Some kind of maya, illusion... There's only one reality. You can't understand their words before you grasp true reality. Until that point, their words remain theories, clever hypotheses.

I laughed. I howled with laughter from deep in my soul, because I'd grasped how fully senseless it is to thirst after enlightenment. It really is funny, because we're all born enlightened, and it makes no sense to wish for what we already have. If you possess something, you can't acquire it. You can only attain that which you don't have, or which is not within you. But enlightenment is within our nature.

Grigory Skovoroda (Ukraine)

Having gotten up early, I went into the garden to have a walk. The first sensation I felt with my heart was a certain unwinding, freedom, cheerfulness, a hope, along with fulfillment. As I directed all my will and desires into this state of my soul, I felt incredible motion within me, which filled me with an incomprehensible strength. An exceedingly sweet illumination instantly filled my soul. It caused all my insides to burst into flame, and it seemed as if a fiery flow was circling through my veins. I began running instead of walking, as if carried by some kind of delight. It didn't feel like I had either arms or legs, but rather as if I was entirely made up of some fiery element borne through the space of this circular existence. The whole world disappeared before me; only a feeling of love, security, peace and eternity gave life to my existence. Tears streamed from my eyes and poured a kind of touching harmony into my whole makeup. I penetrated into myself, sensed the assurance of filial love, and from that moment, I dedicated myself to filial piety to God's spirit.

Elisa Mada Dalian (Canada)

My body began shaking and vibrating in time with the music. Waves of energy began moving up from my feet to my head, and when they reached my Third Eye, they were transformed into light that dispersed in all directions. I was in a state of total release and simply watched what was happening.

Then a giant wave flowed over me, which in the space of a second illuminated my entire body, transforming it into bright light. It felt to me that thousands of suns had suddenly flared up in every cell of my body. The light was blinding, but cool. It seemed like the entire Universe with all its suns and solar systems had suddenly ended up in my body. I was literally swimming in light! A huge Joy filled me, a joy I could describe only as "Absolute blessedness."

The essence that I had known as my "I" suddenly disappeared. Along with the disappearance of the "I" came the realization that the entire Universe lives and breathes within my body. I suddenly saw that all of creation vibrates with Joy, and that this Joy is the byproduct of Creation. I saw that Creation was God himself, who lives in my body and my being, and in all that exists in the Universe. I saw that the source and essence of each person is Joy, and our worldly happiness seemed to me a feeble likeness of the Absolute Joy of Creation that penetrates the whole Universe. I was standing, observing the ignorance of my miniscule ego-mind, when suddenly, out of somewhere in the depths arose a frenzied laugh: how laughable my whole search was, after all, I'd been searching for what I already had. Now I clearly understood how my mind had tried to survive, directing all my attention and efforts toward finding enlightenment outside me, never allowing me to know the truth of what is here in this very moment. I understood that my entire search had been an illusion. I was in the very same place I've been since the very beginning of time. I'd sought enlightenment somewhere outside myself and had busied my mind with that. I myself had finally reached what all mystics have spoken about for centuries: *the path is the goal.* I'd finally returned home.

I found what I'd sought over many lifetimes, and now I had nowhere to go and nothing more to seek. I realized that my being and the Universe were not separate. Now I knew that the very same ecstatic Joy, Light and Love pulsates within everything that exists in the Universe.

Part II

**It's not advisable to read this in a bad mood.
It's highly probable your bad mood will intensify.
It's equally probable that those in possession of a positive outlook
will experience an additional boost of energy and cheerfulness.**

Enlightenment Like It Is

The secret of life lies in "dying before you die" – And in discovering that there is no death.

I avoid using the word "enlightenment." I prefer to use the word "grace." As I noted earlier, many who have a profound meditative or mystical experience might mistakenly call their state enlightenment. Really, a person can use his mind to think up whatever he wants, he can take the false as the true and lead others along a false path. For that reason, I don't use the term "enlightenment" to designate some end point of a spiritual search. Because no end point exists. I don't call myself enlightened, much less someone who's realized the truth. Besides, I'm convinced that enlightenment itself really just does not exist. There does exist a certain state of consciousness in which the ego has been filed down. I say specifically filed *down*, because if it was totally filed away, you'd die. Because it's the ego that supports our life in our physical body. It's my impression that this particular state of consciousness is precisely a state of "grace." It's the state of consciousness in its pure form or, as they say, pure consciousness. It's pure because it simply *is*; external sensations don't enter it via the sense organs, since it's the self-aware form of consciousness, i.e., it has no directionality. In this case consciousness cognizes itself. And it's like a narcissist, totally amazed by itself. By the way, people in this state of consciousness don't really need anyone else. They're happy on their own. They've already realized the secret of life, they've already "died" to passions, desires, and pleasures. They've "died" and realized that death doesn't exist.

Why don't we all possess this kind of consciousness? Why do some people get lucky and wake up and get high on life because they possess this kind of pure consciousness – and by the way, they get high without alcohol, drugs or earthly pleasures – while others root around in their minds and can't manage to exceed its limits, even by drinking?

When a person is born, his stream of consciousness is directed toward getting to know the world around him, the nervous system is gradually retuned, and the person loses the ability to perceive his consciousness in the pure form in which it existed at birth. But it's possible to regain this state. However, it seems to me that it's impossible to do this by using techniques or methods, or by "working on yourself," or through meditation. I tend to think that it is given to us. Although some small percentage of people have gained it through techniques and meditation.

The most ridiculous thing is that some people try to buy this state. There's a whole empire called "spirituality" that's devoted to selling "enlightenment.". These folks sell what they bill as all possible methods you can use to expand your consciousness, techniques and similar nonsense that supposedly will lead you to the land of no suffering. But nobody takes into account the fact that in this suffering-free world, there is simply no one who suffers. While you exist, you'll find everything around you. Once there's no you – there's nothing. It's an instantaneous shift , a quantum leap. It's the state of the wordless witness, or the state of presence. The witness doesn't do anything, it just observes its life without judgment, dissatisfaction or doubts. You'll always remain in a state free of becoming entangled in all that's going on around you. This is also called internal freedom, a feeling of gratification, peace, liberation from the tyranny of the mind, understanding, truth. It's not important what we call it. What's important is getting there. Many people will ask, why do we even need that, why try to get there? Just the act of reaching this state of consciousness won't do anything for you as a person. It won't make you smarter, more successful or richer. But you'll gain something far greater – freedom, true freedom. Many confuse this with false freedom: I can do what I want, do where I want, allow myself to have everything I want, fulfill all my desires. That's it's own kind of freedom, but a false freedom, because it's a trap. This kind of freedom will take you around in circles, you're like a hamster in a wheel, running from one desire to the next. You'll feel no sense that you need to take responsibility for your own life. Real freedom is freedom from the desires which our mind foists upon us, freedom from its tyranny, freedom from the false individual, from the false "I" which wants and which, when it gets what it wants, then suffers, grows ill, and dies. It's wisdom. In real life, the awakened person is the most ordinary person. He or she could be your neighbor or your coworker. You're not likely to recognize him. Sometimes a glance will give him away, the way he seems to be looking out from deep inside. Living within this state is very simple. Being awakened is the true nature of any spiritual being, i.e, of you and me. It's immutable, eternal and endless. Everything changes, everything except our primordial nature, which we've simply forgotten. That's why enlightenment is accessible to absolutely any individual. It's already within us! We only have to do one small thing: free ourselves from the illusions our mind has created.

One day a friend said to me, "People who crave enlightenment are so foolish." I have to note that she's both a yoga instructor and a guru for many seekers. "People are fools, because they lose valuable time by searching. I don't need enlightenment. I like to enjoy life, I take pleasure in my body and in all that surrounds me. When I'm happy, I totally dissolve in that, and when I'm sad, then I'm present with that, too." My friend chose the totality approach. That's one of the methods offered by Advaita. I accept her position, but I don't entirely share it. Learning to accept life as striped, like a zebra, where you fully delight in the light stripe and are also totally present when the dark appears – that's great, but it's not the final point on the journey. Lots of people even achieve a kind of high and think that this striped life is a given. I'm feeling bad now, but everything will pass. Tomorrow's a new day. They're always in the future when they feel bad, and always in terror when they feel good, afraid of losing the good. In this way sufferings are exchanged for delight, a bitter taste replaces pleasure. And this process is endless, it all goes round and round and repeats again and again. I don't hold with what my friend teaches her students, not at all. In her groups, along with yoga, you develop your extrasensory abilities, your paranormal capacities, clairvoyance, you practice leaving your body. People like experiencing success in these areas, experiencing meditative states. People flock to her, craving miracles, she has a lot of students, and they're all moving along in some direction. Just where that is, I don't know, but I've noticed that the further along they go, the stronger their ego gets. Their spiritual ego grows stronger. "I can do this, I'm not like everyone else, I can leave my body" and so on. All these paranormal phenomena are a pure waste of time. They're a road to nowhere. They can't lead you to the quantum leap I'm writing about. For that you need the state of mind in which all the "cockroaches" in your mind have been exterminated as thoroughly as possible. That's when something can happen. Or maybe it won't, that depends on luck. The experience of many awakened ones shows that a large factor in all of this is being close to, having actual in person contact with people who are bearers of this state (enlightenment, awakening.) For reasons we don't entirely understand, simply being in their presence can have an effect, if the person is ready. The awakened one serves as a catalyst, gives you the jolt that makes it possible for "the final barrier" in perception to collapse. This is the way it's happened in the majority of the instances of enlightenment of which we're aware.

For this reason, I advise you not to spend money on fake teachers, or on all possible classes about the right way to live, or on life coaches. All of these are of just fleeting value. In the larger scheme of things, when a person's first setting out on a spiritual path, he doesn't need anyone. He's fully capable of beginning to work on himself. Depending on how much work he does, how he matures, and how necessary it is for him to go further, he'll find someone who will show him the way. The teacher will appear if the student is ready. And this teacher doesn't necessarily have to be some cool, popular master from India. It can be a person with whom you feel a connection. The main thing is to sense that connection. But unfortunately, we're used to worshiping authorities, so we usually accept only the people with the big names. But really, this is has to do with each individual's openness. In actual fact, in recent times more and more people on our planet have been experiencing awakening. Why is that happening? I don't know, probably it's because the world is ready for a quantum leap, for the new consciousness so many people have been talking about lately. For this reason, you don't have to do much searching for these folks. You come across them in your travels, there's more than a few of them around, although they're still rare, of course. But they're always nearby right when you need them. In the course of the last two years, fate has brought me together with several such people, and that was on different continents and it happened without any effort whatsoever on my part. Unfortunately, I've never been to India, so I haven't met a single guru there. Although one of those gurus happened to be visiting the very same city in Russia on the very day I was also there. Wouldn't you call that a miracle?

The First Stage of Spiritual Work

Everything I mention here refers only to the beginning of your search. If you're already on the path of awakening, you can skip several chapters. They're for those in whom the fire has yet to be lit. If the candle's burning inside you, then there's no way to extinguish it. That's the way it works, that if you've already set out on the Path, you can't put an end to the Path. No matter how hard we might try to do this, no matter what circumstances are working against us, it's nonetheless impossible to suspend the search for wisdom. The spiritual work will continue. Although teachers will exhort you not to search, to let go of the search, to give up, your inner "I" will still keep digging up everything that's buried underneath your mind. If you do manage to set your search aside, it'll only be for a short time, and it will usually happen out of weakness.

So, on the first stage of spiritual work it's crucial to figure out what your priorities are. Where do you place your focus, as an individual? Think about what your life revolves around. Where do your core priorities lie? Here you need to grasp the following concept: if you're focused more on material things and you usually make decisions based on common sense, then you'll definitely achieve success in your life. You'll plant numerous trees, you'll gain a reasonable level of success in society, as well as the respect of those around you. It's possible that you'll make a good career for yourself, will achieve prestige, and will earn a lot of money. But inside you'll entirely lose out, because you'll never come to know yourself, never come to know that stillness, that depth that is inherent within all of us. You already possess it, you need only stretch your hand out to it.   Stillness, peace, goodness, eternal happiness, unconditional love, grace, call it what you like, it exists within every person.   To see it, you need only refocus your attention. And once you do that, there's no way back - at that point the candle's already lit.   But it's impossible to refocus if you don't have your priorities straight in your life.

Setting your priorities in life is an especially personal matter for each of us.   Racing to accumulate material prosperity also has its advantages.   A person sets goals for himself, reaches them, and expends energy doing so.   He's barely managed to satisfy one desire, when another arises to take its places, and the person dives into the abyss of this new chase. And there's no end to it.   Once he's successful one time, a person feels drawn immediately to succeed again.   The first desire is replaced by a new one, and the person's off and running for his whole life.   He's always occupied with this.   But in the grand scheme of things, everyone attains the same kind of successes.   At age 4, it's considered a success if you don't pee in your pants, at 12, it's if you have friends, at 20, it's if you're having sex, at 35, it's if you're making a decent living, at 60, it's if you're still having sex, at 70, it's if you still have friends, and at 80, it's if you're still not peeing in your pants. Many people think this is the meaning of life, they call this "life's charm" and its passions.   But believe me, this isn't at all what true charm, true delight are about.   The true delight and goodness of our existence on earth lie not in possessing, but in giving.   If your priorities still lie on the material end of things, then perhaps you've picked up this book in error.   If that's the case, you're better off arming yourself with literature on personal growth, with books that will teach you how to make your wishes come true, with advice about how to earn a million dollars, and so on. Overall, nearly all of contemporary psychology (with the exception of a few different offshoots) is oriented toward fulfilling desires, toward comfort and prosperity. In this book you won't find advice about how to acquire this or that tasty morsel. What you will find are the first steps you can take toward freeing yourself of them. Working on your false "I", which thirsts only to receive, working on your egoism, which only keeps us from achieving love – it's a large task and a large sacrifice. And at the beginning stage you won't be getting any carrots. Only sticks. When you go to a session with a psychologist (of course, not all of them work this way, there are some psychologists who have really gone deeply into their own work) more often than not, he starts trying to build up your false "I." In other words, all your "crap" gets covered over with roses, your self-esteem gets raised up, they suggest that you're the most this and the most that, and after therapy you really do come out smelling differently, with a desire to set goals, to repent and to make an effort. But therapy is temporary. After some time you go to a therapist for another session, because the roses have faded, and the "crap" has risen to the surface again, in the form of depression, despondency, lack of desire to live, and so on. Once you discover your false "I" and begin the subsequent work on it, at first you won't be able to soar in winged flight or smell like a rose. It will be painful to dig around in the falsity. This is not a path for the weak. But this is the path to full recovery, and what becomes your main criterion here is love. Once you start working with some of the methods I present later on, it's possible that you might experience depression. How deep it gets will depend on the extent to which falsity has overgrown your character. Some people manage to build up so many unnecessary barriers in the course of their life and cultivate so many unneeded work-arounds and illusions in their heads, that when the realization dawns that they're unnecessary, then depression sets in, a reluctance to part with what's familiar, comfortable. After all, something new always frightens us, even if it's incommensurably more important.

The Second Stage of Spiritual Work

If above I suggested you take a look at your life from a distance and judge what's at its center and where your life's priorities lie, then now I'll attempt to explain why we need to make changes. If a person is satisfied with everything, has no problems in his life, has no physical or mental illness, experiences no suffering or pain, then we can say that he's got his priorities straight, including how he views material things. That means he isn't hooked by money, because if he were, then he wouldn't have it; he isn't hooked by earthly goods, because otherwise he'd have been deprived of them; he isn't hooked by anything else, which means that nothing is separating this person from the divine, that he hasn't built up any barriers around himself. But you don't meet such people very often. The majority of people are dissatisfied with their lives, they suffer and they are ill. For this reason, when you're at the second stage of spiritual work, it's important to understand that you can't help but move from focusing on material (non-enduring, non-stable, empty) pleasure to cultivating spiritual and emotional (eternal, real, unshakeable) happiness in yourself. No matter what, your soul will have to endure a period of renouncing the material for the sake of achieving the spiritual. Sooner or later it will find it can't escape facing the necessity of changing. Like it or not, a person will have to make this shift, and he won't want to do it willingly, he'll have to be forced to do it. He'll be forced into it by unpleasant circumstances in his life. That's the way it frequently happens. A person flits around like a butterfly until about the age of 25 to 30. He doesn't have a care in the world, everything comes together for him, he has lots of energy. After thirty you notice a decline. Maybe bad things start to happen, maybe your personal life falls apart or you have some bad luck at work. It takes more effort for you to accomplish things than it did before thirty. Why does that happen? Because all this time you've been moving in the wrong direction. Not toward love, which gives you energy, but toward the material, which only exhausts your energy. It's after age thirty that people usually experience profound despondency for the first time. Despondency is one of the symptoms of low energy. Secondary symptoms of decreased energy include envy, regret, and dissatisfaction with yourself. Egotism becomes your whole mode of operation in life. You're interested only in yourself. Recall what you were like when you were young. Young people don't usually feel regret or dissatisfaction in regard to themselves. And even if they do feel envy, it's usually short-lived, momentary. People are full of energy for moving ahead and achieving. That's no longer the case after age thirty. And the problem has to do not with age, but with a lost connection to the Divine. If a person doesn't move toward love of his own free will, then the energy is cut off and the difficulties begin. When trouble strikes, that's the most opportune time to review our life's values and priorities. That's the only way we can get a glimpse of the truth. And whether we start moving toward truth and love or remain in the darkness depends entirely on us. Whether we'll greet old age in happiness and peace or, ailing, pester our children and grandchildren to give a drop of attention to this decrepit person we're becoming. By the way, illness is another one of those beacons of light that can illuminate something within us, teach us how to understand ourselves, help us turn ourselves in the necessary direction. But again, this is possible only if we view the illness correctly and approach it the right way. But that's another story.

The Third Stage of Spiritual Work

If your priorities in life don't tend toward the material, you'll definitely come to realize that sooner or later, and when you do, that's when your true life begins. At this moment your view of things changes. You understand that you can't get anywhere this way – material benefits can't give you all that your soul is striving for. They simply don't bring you pleasure any more, and your life seems empty and uninteresting. Of course, it's at this stage of life – when a person has truly made some profound discoveries, but still hasn't made his choice –that the real war between Light and Dark begins on some battlefield we can't even see. It often happens that when people intuitively sense something more meaningful, when they come to understand that the material side of life is of secondary importance, then they begin filling up the ensuing emptiness with alcohol, narcotics and depraved behavior. One gets the sense that the dark forces are doing all they can to keep a person from going to the side of the Light.

For that reason, at this stage of your work, you'll need courage, fortitude and strength of will. When the pointlessness of material benefits and of your ego hits you, when a sincere need to grow and move in the direction of unconditional love arises, but when you're as of yet without a strong foundation – and still lack sufficient fire and the necessary mental state – you might possibly experience terrible depression. At this point, nothing interests you any more. But the new foundation hasn't formed yet. So here begins an unstable period of wandering, of throwing yourself into one religion after the next, the period of searching for God. But this is a necessary period. At this stage there's no point in filling the empty spot in your life with a series of empty "toys." You'll just get sick of that. It's at this very stage that all possible methods and techniques for spiritual growth really can be a big help to the seeker. It could be Christian prayer, ointments, meditation, yoga, Vipassana, techniques for coming to know yourself, and so on. Again, whichever you pick is up to you, depending on your own psychological needs. During this period, it's important not to fall under the sway of false teachers and religious leaders of various stripes. Because no one knows you better than you know yourself. When you begin this work, it's useful to observe your body and your thoughts. For example, it's very easy notice that your body adopts a comfortable pose or turns over when you're lying down before you're even consciously aware of wanting to do that. In other words, you're not thinking about whether or not you should turn onto your right side or remain on your left. You do it without thinking. Other observations along these lines will quickly lead you to the awareness that you are not your body. That your body is much wiser. It's capable of doing everything correctly without the mind's participation, and more quickly than a command can come from the mind. More precisely, our nervous system will respond to a command from the brain so quickly that the mind can't keep up with it, it's in no state to keep track of the path by which the command is actually carried out. Later on, when you're watching your thoughts, you'll have the realization that thoughts fly into your head all on their own, without you participating in the process at all. You can't do a thing with them! Along with this realization comes the understanding that you are not your mind. So what are you? Maybe you're your feelings, your emotions? So at this point it makes sense to observe how your emotions are expressed. Are you capable of controlling them? It's possible, but only for a short time, and usually at the expense of your own health. It's been proven long ago that holding onto an insult leads to inflammation, that insult combined with ill will which steals into your insides leads to cancer, etc. So, things aren't so simple in regard to emotions, either. They're outside your control. Then what really is truly yours, what belongs to you? You don't control your body, you control your mind even less, and whether you control your emotions is also largely in question. So what are you then? The moment you pose this question, your journey into yourself begins.

Who am I and what can I do?

In order to be yourself you have to know for sure who you aren't.

One of the awakened beings from the last century, Gopala Krishnamurti, said somewhere that the most senseless and foolish question in the world is the question, "Who am I?" That's because it's impossible to answer it by using your mind. The answer comes when the mind is calm, when all thoughts recede into the background, when you're not entangled in the process, when you are nothing but a Witness. But at that point no questions arise, especially not foolish ones. It's fairly complicated to calm your mind. A disturbed mind wants to know everything and is constantly asking questions. And it's looking for the answers, too. There's no point in even trying to halt this thought process. It's impossible, and you don't need to; that's an empty and useless waste of time. The thoughts themselves – and you're not their author – can't hinder you in your spiritual search. What hinders you is becoming emotionally entangled in the process, your desires. We're used to rooting around in all the garbage in our heads, to being under the thumb of our thoughts and desires. So, day and night, we have no peace. Even as we sleep, we continue to dream. Even at night we act in various ways, negotiate deals, have conversations, think. We give ourselves credit for something, we're proud of our successes and feel disheartened if something's not going right. To put it succinctly, we act as if we're the authors of everything. But the answer to this question of our authorship is entirely debatable. We can't even be sure whether we'll be able to go to the bathroom tomorrow, or whether we'll be beset by constipation. So how can we be convinced that our designs will be realized? Unfortunately, our seeming authorship is born of our habit of thinking of ourselves as separate, independently existing beings. We fully equate ourselves with our ideas, with thought. So the first thing we need to do is to realize that we are no one. We are supporting actors who've gotten a false sense of ourselves as the authors and controllers of our fates. Even though in reality we're powerless to change anything, even in our own lives, much less in the lives of other people. Sure, it's easy for us to butt into others' lives and cause harm, we're big experts at that, but we're incapable of changing anything on a fundamental level. It goes without saying that we have freedom of choice, but we have no freedom *from* choice. And that means that we always make the very choice we're obliged to make. We take the actions we're obliged to take. All our acts take place automatically. Our nervous system contains a large number of programs that determine everything, determine absolutely all our behavior. Absolutely all of our life. And the only way we can affect anything in our life is to gain an understanding of our own personal programs. It's useless to fight them, but we can update and improve them. But before you can do that, you have to catch a glimpse of the programs. And just attaining this vision is more than enough to change your life for the better. Now I'll talk about how to do that.

If we spend a little time observing people, we'll notice that all their movements, their thoughts, actions, their words, phrases and events repeat. And they are all predictable. People play out the same scenarios time and again. They fall into the same traps time and again. They're robots. And you're a robot, too. You're just a more complex model, but a robot all the same, as am I.

So it's very, very doubtful that we're the authors of our lives. For example, a thought arises in our mind, and a moment later, our ego says, "I thought that." The mind solves problems, but then the ego says, "What a wonderful solution I found!" Based on the mind's decisions, the body carries out actions, but all the while the ego says, "I did that." In reality, all of this is the will of God Most High, God, Allah, Lord – it doesn't matter what names different religions give him. The games consciousness plays and the presence of ego are also His Will. And the disappearance of all the games and illusions when you work on yourself – that's also God's Will. The fact that you're reading this book – that's His Will, too. Whether you start working on your self or don't start – it's God's Will. Whether this understanding arises in you now, or whether it never arises at all – it's God's Will. Whether you achieve enlightenment or grace in this lifetime, or don't achieve it – that's God's Will. If some force has compelled us to take up the question of self-inquiry, then sooner or later that force will carry that process out to its end – to self-knowing. The idea that "nothing depended on me, depends on me or will depend on me" definitely doesn't appeal much to many people. After all, we prefer to have the illusion of freedom of choice. It's more interesting to live that way, the ego keeps on playing – it wants to survive, try on various masks, have a good time. But it's impossible to live this way without identifying with the masks, without buying into the illusions. For this reason, many people who have become tightly bound, who are prisoners of desire and of their own ego, will certainly say, "That's a good thought, but it's nonsense! A person forges his own fate. All is in his hands." That's just one more big illusion and ego game. Because without its illusions, the mind has nothing to keep it busy. The idea that there's no freedom of choice hits the ego below the belt. When I hinted to one of my friends – a woman who had a bunch of problems in her personal life and who was incapable of making any decisions – that she'd be better off relaxing and trusting in God, this is what she said: "You think I should do nothing? If we don't have any choice, then we're just marionettes. I don't want to be a marionette. I need to see the logic in everything that happens around me. I can't do nothing and just wait to see where I'll wash up. What, are we supposed to be like shit that floats along without knowing what sewer it'll be flushed into?" This person wasn't ready to be a marionette, even in divine hands. She wanted to be the master of her own fate. Anyone with such a giant ego will probably end up suffering a lot before he gains understanding and a profound acceptance of all that is, before his individual authorship disappears and merging can occur. But what can you do? Each person has his own path and no one else can travel it for him.

Actually, there's nothing so scary about having all these illusions and games in your head, or the sense that you're the author of your fate. After all, that's also God's Will. The more you observe yourself, the deeper you go into studying yourself, the more the illusions will disperse, and one by one the walls that keep us separate, keep us from merging with the Creator, will fall away, and only the Truth will remain. It's just that for now, we're unable to trust in life (in God's Will) because we fear that suddenly something will go "not the way I want it to". After all, we have our beliefs about how things should happen, how the world should be, how we should be in that world. We need to free ourselves from these convictions as soon as possible, because they make it impossible for us to achieve self-knowledge and go further. They put the brakes on us.

Methods for Spiritual Growth

> **One monk says to the elder monk:**
> **"It's hard to see where our duty lies."**
> **"On the contrary, it's easy," answers the elder.**
> **"Our duty is what we feel least like doing."**

There are several methods that can help us free ourselves from our beliefs, reset our programs, or more precisely, free ourselves from their influence. (Or, they might not help us – everyone's different, and it all depends on the Will of the God Most High.) In the next chapter I introduce one of these methods, one that is a tremendous help in clearing the garbage out of your "hut." By "hut" I mean the mind, which is chock full of all possible conceptions that taken together make up our approach to life. A flawed approach leads to mistakes, unpleasant experiences, disease, suffering. A right approach to life and correct life's priorities lead to a happy fate and to the absence of suffering. And I'll remind you that all these various methods, including this dualities method that I'll talk about below, can be helpful at the beginning of your path. They can help clear your mind of unnecessary trash, sweep everything out of your hut, and open all its windows, so you can just live. If you prepare your hut in this way, it's more likely that something can fly in, something called Love, Truth, Understanding, Grace. Although I'm convinced that these things are simply given to us. And not necessarily to those who are seeking and waiting for them. More often than not, it's to those who aren't looking or waiting at all. You can meditate in a lotus position for years or practice Vipassana and still not experience any profound changes at all. There's no technique that can give a person what he's seeking as long as there's still someone seeking. Who's seeking? Our mind, of course. So, once again, it's leading us by the nose.

But all the same, techniques can help us dismantle our stereotypes of thought and behavior, our mental limits, the barriers, incorrect views of life, fears, discomforts and beliefs that keep us from living "here and now," keep us from enjoying life in each of its moments. The techniques can reduce our suffering, free us from negative thoughts, help us establish right priorities in our life. I'll describe several such techniques below. I've tested them all on myself, they're all absolutely safe, and give very quick results. There's no reason to fear that these techniques will somehow affect or wipe out our functional mind, the one that controls our organism's vital activities. No, it's impossible to wipe that out. But the emotional mind, which keeps us from enjoying life, i.e., the mind that makes value judgments, judges, labels, gets drawn into occurrences, compares, sets impossible tasks for us, creates problems, continually demands something and is eternally dissatisfied – you can wipe out that one, if not entirely, then at least partly, which will noticeably improve your life and save you a lot of money in the bargain, money you would have spent on therapists and psychologists. Of course, you need more than just techniques to achieve this. You also need two other things, to a lesser degree: you have to be ready, and you need a teacher. But even if you use just these techniques and do nothing else, they'll noticeably weaken and undermine your emotional mind and in that way make your life more joyful. I described one of the techniques, "the Dalian Meditation," earlier. The techniques I offer below are suitable for practically anyone, since you can do them at any time, on your own, without any financial expenditure. However, just like any other techniques, you have to approach them in the right way. The dualities technique should categorically not be undertaken by anyone who is psychologically unstable. Please, before you try it, read the following information carefully.

Warning

The reader accepts *full and unconditional* responsibility for the use, understanding and application of the techniques presented here. More detailed information and free consultations concerning the techniques are available at http://www.pro-svet.at.ua. All of these techniques have been tested by the author of this book and by other seekers over the course of many years.

However, none of the techniques introduced here are recommended for independent use by people who are in poor physical, mental, emotional or psychological condition. The following categories of people are prohibited from using the given techniques: pregnant women, nursing mothers, minors; those who have in the past attempted suicide or who have a tendency toward suicidal thoughts; those with a tendency toward violence or cruelty; as well as those with an unstable psyche and/or uncontrollable behavior. Such people should consult with the appropriate specialists.

If you are currently, or have been under the care of a psychologist, psychotherapist, psychiatrist and/or other similar specialists, if you have had classes/sessions/healings of any type, if you've taken anti-depressants and want to use the material in this book for independent work on yourself, you should consult with these specialists before doing so.

In the course of working on yourself using these techniques, you should drink a lot of water; not use narcotics, alcohol, medicines or preparations that act on the nervous system and brain; eat well and get a sufficient amount of sleep, and also engage in as much physical activity as supports a regular feeling of good health.

Due to the strength and effectiveness of these techniques, disregarding *any* of the previous points can lead to unexpected and negative results!

If you are not prepared to accept full responsibility for your current and future state, please do not practice the given techniques. Read this book only as my autobiography.

There's no point in taking up all the techniques one right after the other. It's better to pick one that suits you most and focus on it – one that "works" for you – and practice that one consistently.

Dualities Technique

> A girl is pulling the petals off a daisy:
> "He loves me, he loves me not, he loves me, he
> love me not, he loves me, he loves me not..."
> There are only three petals left: "he loves me,
> he loves me not, ... oh, crap."

Working with dualities is one of my favorite topics. At one point it significantly cleared out my garbage-filled mind and helped me progress further. It comes from a Russian researcher who has devoted himself to the Path for more than ten years. You can read about it in more detail at http://www.pro-svet.at.ua.

Studying dualities allows us to normalize our worldview in a short time, free ourselves from our stagnant conceptions, values, attachments, from all that keeps us from moving toward the Light, sensing the Light and unity with the Universe, and from delighting in life in all its manifestations in every moment.

Here are several rules that will help you receive maximum benefit:

1. Get enough sleep. 7 ½-9 hours is usually sufficient.
2. Don't use substances that negatively affect the nervous system, brain and consciousness. You can make an exception for tea and coffee, if you can't get along without them. If you have been using alcohol, pain relievers, narcotics or other similar substances, wait 1-10 days, until their effects have entirely ceased.
3. Eat a healthy diet and drink a lot of water.
4. Make sure that nothing and no one will distract you while working with dualities. Set aside an hour or more.
5. Once you begin working with dualities, work through the technique all the way to the end. Don't start the second

one if you haven't finished the first – it can be painful.

6. Before you begin this work, make sure that you fully understand how to do the technique and what you might expect in the course of your practice and afterwards.

7. If you start to feel bad while doing the work, take a short break, drink some water, get some fresh air, shift your attention to the room or to the view outside, and understand that you've become *overloaded* with the contents of your mind and subconscious. Don't resist this material, don't avoid it, don't ignore it; just allow it to come out and accept it as it is – it will disperse all on its own. When you begin to feel better, continue your work from where you left off, and finish it.

8. Before you begin working on a given topic, drink a glass of water and exercise until you develop a light sweat.

Duality is a pair of total opposites (polarities, poles) in the human mind. For example, good and evil, love and hate, good and bad. There are a great number of dualities, and each of us has our own individual collection of dualities that exist only for us personally.

But there are several common dualities that come into play for all of us to a greater or lesser extent.

All these dualities exist only in the human mind. One pole of the pair is opposite to the other (it complements it, balances it), but only in the human mind.

The entire mind (including the subconscious) is constructed on the basis of dualities. All concepts in the human mind have their opposites. This is often expressed simply by adding negation. For example "should I buy a newspaper or not buy a newspaper," "should I get married or not get married," "should I move to a new house or not move to a new house."

You need to understand that if a given duality feels charged to you, then that's because you've constructed it yourself, or consented to it (you've agreed that it has a place in your mind.) Consenting to a duality means creating it for yourself. It's your creation, even if you were forced or convinced to create it. For that reason, **never forget that you yourself are the creator of all dualities.** Remembering that will hasten your work. When you work through a duality, you go outside the boundaries of the dualistic mind.

Everything that exists in the mind (and the subconscious) is held there only by the existence of dualities. Dualities are the foundation atop which our life experience accumulates. That's how the mind is constructed.

When you work with dualities' end points (their polarities) you affect **all** the material that exists between them, too. That's the most effective way.

There are charged dualities, ones that disturb you, as well as not so charged dualities. As a rule, people don't see that these are dualities, because they're interested in only one pole of the duality. For example, a person wants to become free (of something) and that means that the charged polarity for him is "to be free." He gets that. But he doesn't see the flip side of duality (the one he creates *without realizing it)* – "not to be free." After all, in order to move toward freedom, you need a pole away from which to move. It is created automatically (subconsciously); and the more strongly a person wants freedom, then the more unfree he makes himself (subconsciously.) **Otherwise he wouldn't be able to move toward the opposite pole.** The charge (the tension, the negative) between the poles grows, and the duality's effect on consciousness increases, suppressing common sense, so that the person suffers as a result. (Various religions, organizations, sects and the like make a fortune based on this.) So, in the given example, let's say the duality "to be free – not to be free" has a charge for someone. They need to work both ends of the duality. **Working with only one of the extremes is less effective, because you're not touching both of the two end points that support everything. An unresolved end point retains its polar opposite.**

You won't be able to remove only one pole and leave the other, because they support each other. For this reason, while you're working with one pole, work with the other, too. Work with the poles in an alternating fashion: 1, 2, 1, 2, etc. Working this way will yield a stronger effect than working on the poles separately. It depends on you to constantly switch the focus of your work (your position) and not get stuck at one pole or the other. This gives you more space to view the situation, and you'll move outside of the boundaries of the mind more quickly.

The key is to alternately create and remove the poles through your attention to each. For example:

1. Create the idea that _____ (pole 1) and hold it in your mind.
2. Create the idea that _____ (pole 2) and hold it in your mind.

"Create the idea" means to make this idea real for yourself, *or*, to think this thought. It's desirable to *hold* it for at least several seconds, which at the beginning can seem an extremely difficult task – that's because material from the past will bubble up, material connected in some way to the pole you're holding. As you near the end of your work with the given duality, you'll be able to hold the poles easily without any unpleasant sensations – nothing more will bubble up.

While holding the idea in your mind, strive to feel it as fully as you can!

We switch back and forth from pole 1 to pole 2, from 1 to 2, from 1 to 2, and so on, accepting any garbage our mind tosses out just as it is, and we keep going until we reach the ultimate result.

This is a very simple technique for working with dualities, but also pretty powerful. It is perfectly suited for the majority of dualities.

Examples of dualities:

1. Create the idea that you're special.
2. Create the idea that you're just like everyone else.

Or:

1. Create the idea that fate exists.
2. Create the idea that there's no fate.

Or:

1. Create the idea that you're responsible for everything in your life.
2. Create the idea that you are not responsible for anything.

Or:

1. I want a new job.
2. I don't want a new job.

And so on, depending on what is most charged for you at this point in your life.

Note: When you're creating an idea, strive to endow it with as much conviction as you can – it's more effective that way. For example, if you're creating the idea "fate exists," then that thought should sound convincing, without any doubts. Then, "there is no fate" should be just as convincing, too.

Work with the first pole, then the second, then the first again, then the second, until you achieve the end result.

When the material that exists between the two poles is wiped out (discharged) the duality disappears. What does that mean? It means that it ceases to have significance for you. It no longer disturbs you. On the level of understanding, of course, the two poles remain, and you can distinguish one from the other analytically, but now the material that was once between the poles and which affected you negatively, is no longer present. But you need to work only with those dualities that carry a charge for you.

At first, working with dualities can seem a bit unpleasant and protracted – a lot of material of various types will float up that isn't particularly connected to the duality you're working on. This could be unpleasant emotions or thoughts, images, entire episodes from your life, etc. You need to expect that this will happen, and no one's saying it will always be easy. But in order to transcend the boundaries of the dual mind once and for all, you have to go through all of this.

The effects of freeing yourself from all of this are cumulative, and the further you go, the easier it will be. The beginning stage is the most difficult of all. Those who aren't up to it will get weeded out right away and will go busy themselves with something more pleasant and useless, such as going to a spa or finding a new shoulder to cry on. And that's the way it should be. This path is not for everyone.

Yawning, sleepiness, fogginess of mind – these are all signs that negative material is working its way to the conscious level. You may not always recognize the material as concrete incidents from the past, but that's not necessary. You may experience only sensations, such as heaviness or discomfort in your body, and there may be unpleasant emotions, thoughts, etc.

There will also be **pleasant sensations** that come up, usually **when you finish working with a concrete duality.** They might last a long time or not very long. This depends on various factors.

The result you're looking for when working through a duality is that you no longer feel any tension when you consider the duality and either of its poles. There's a feeling of peace, lightness, and relaxation. Ideally, you'll be able to hold both poles in your mind at once without discomfort, without preferring either one of them *at that moment* (although at first this doesn't always happen.) Often, but not always, when you finish working with a duality, **laughter** will arise (as one of the indicators that something negative has been discharged.) You may experience various other **pleasant sensations and emotions,** such as **joy, a burst of energy, a feeling of liberation, emptiness** (where previously you sensed a problem) and so on. A new understanding of a situation or the solution to a problem may also arise. Once you attain the result you're looking for, it's time to end your work with the duality in question. The rule is: **ALWAYS WORK ONLY WITH DUALITIES THAT ARE CHARGED FOR YOU.**

How to find the dualities that are charged for you. In order to do this, ask yourself a series of questions such as:

- What's important to me?

- What do I want?

- What do I fear?

- What disturbs me?

- What do I want to change in my life?

- What do I think about myself?

- What do I think about others? (about any given person or groups, organizations, etc.)

- What do I think about my own life? (and the lives of others, if this is important to you)

- What do I think about the past?

And so on.

As you answer one of these concrete questions, you'll discover one pole. In order to find the complete duality, you'll have to select its opposite, the opposing pole. Both poles of the duality should carry some charge for you, "hook you", elicit a reaction! What counts as a reaction is any variety of **NON-acceptance of what is**.

As you answer the questions that come to you, you'll discover a multitude of your beliefs. Any belief or judgment has its opposite, with which it forms a duality, and you process this the way you'd process any other duality. You won't be able to fully settle your accounts with a conviction without touching on its opposite.

How can you find a duality? Let's say that in answer to the question, "What do I want?" I answer, "I want to have my own business." So, "I want to have my own business" becomes one half of my charged duality. Now I need to find the second, polar opposite, the counterbalancing half. Often it's formed through negation, by adding negative particles such as "not, don't, isn't." And so I end up with this duality: "I want to have my own business – I don't want to have my own business." Before setting to work on this duality, I need to make sure I've stated it correctly. It might be more accurate to put it this way: "I intend to have my own business – I intend not to have my own business." They have different shades of meaning, so pick the more accurate one. **Take care to make sure that the second pole is absolutely opposite in meaning to the first.** "I want to have my own business – I don't *really* want to have my own business" isn't a correct wording, since the second pole isn't totally opposite to the first in meaning (it's somewhere between the two end points.) **An incorrectly worded duality will give you fewer results, or even no results.**

Everything that is charged for you can be worded as a duality and processed.

A LIST OF DUALITIES

Moses said everything comes from God
Solomon said everything comes from the head
Christ said everything comes from the heart
Marx said everything comes from the stomach
Freud said everything comes from sex
But Einstein said everything is relative

And so, once you've answered these questions for yourself and have **put together a written list of your dualities** (I strongly recommend doing this) choose the one that's most charged for you (the one that disturbs or interests you) and begin working with it. Over time new dualities will expand your list, and old ones you've processed with be crossed off. Each time, choose the most charged duality and work with that one.

Even just making up and adding to your list can have a therapeutic effect, since it allows you to see the whole picture as a collection of dualities rather than of separate poles. You'll immediately sense the difference, and that will be useful. What's more, this list will remain in your mind; and when, in the course of your life, you come up against one of the poles from your list, you'll also see the opposite pole, which will help keep you from introversion, from getting stuck in one of the poles.

To find the dualities that are charged for you personally, you can use the provided lists of dualities that you'll find in various practices. Sometimes that's helpful. However, remember that you should work only with the one that feels charged to you, rather than with all of them one after the other. There's no sense in working through some endless lists of dualities, especially if you think you *should* work through a certain sequence of them. Everyone's different, and there's simply no one correct set of lists.

Laying them out on paper will help you get a better sense of your individual dualities. Take a sheet of paper and divide it in half with a vertical line. Above the first column write one pole, and above the second column write the second pole. Draw a horizontal line below them.

Then, below each pole, describe it, in as much detail as possible. As if you were trying to explain to a child what each polar opposite meant. Write down what meaning it has **for you.** How important, key, grandiose, repulsive or undesirable, etc., it is.

Now make another horizontal line under your description of the poles.

Next, under each pole, write down absolutely all that's connected with it for you: emotions, thoughts, plans, decisions, expectations, unexpected events, goals, successes, failures, experiences, people, realizations, and so on. As a rule, at the beginning, material will surface all on its own, and all you need to do is take it and write it down. You don't need to filter anything – no one's going to read it. Your job is to draw out EVERYTHING connected to each pole.

Do your best to fill both columns out equally. Do this until you reach the expected result. Once you've exhausted all the material, you can destroy the sheets of paper.

These techniques won't "clean out" all dualities 100%, but they will do a good job of purging the negative.

The "Right Now Is All I Have" Technique

Don't take everything in life. Take everything in full.

Our mind is constructed in such a way that it's always pulling us either into the past or the future. Observe your thoughts and you'll easily be convinced that this is the case. The mind needs time – it's the only way it can maintain control over a situation. In the moment "now", the mind doesn't have any sense of time. For this reason, if you try to be in the "now", you'll quickly see that doing so is not so simple. The mind is constantly darting to the past and then to the present. What's more, you'll find being in the now a rather boring activity. The mind will start wanting "entertainment" – either some memories, or some plans for the future. In the present moment, it's powerless, there's nothing for it to do here, and so it immediately draws you either to the past or future. Because in the present moment, the mind has no need of anything. Try using "thinking" about the past or future only when it's really necessary for the present, when it's necessary in order to carry out practical tasks. For example, it's totally normal to return to the past if you want to remember something you need right now, or to head off into the future in order to come up with a plan for your present moment actions. But to putter around in the past so you can replay your endless conversations with others, to replay a tape of events gone by is not only an idle activity, but harmful, too, since it helps you hold on to and accumulate pain. As well, when we keep turning our attention to past events, we age more quickly. The more the past weighs us down, the more quickly we age. Eckhart Tolle, the marvelous explorer of man's essence, wrote in his book, "In each moment, die to the past. You don't need it. Feel the power of the now and the oneness of Being. Sense your presence."

Constant thinking about the past is nothing more than not accepting it. Pain and suffering in the present also always represent your non-acceptance. And it can be unconscious non-acceptance, too. It seems to you that you accept everything, that you're okay with everything, you've forgiven everyone, you're satisfied with everything and aren't resisting the least little bit, all at the same time as your mind keeps leading you back to the past over and over, or paints pictures of a future that will definitely be better than the present. And if fear is present – and it usually is – then your mind will definitely paint the future in threatening colors. If the future comes and it's different from the way your mind described it – you'll experience pain, and if everything's okay, you'll still feel pain, because the mind will once again carry you off to the future or will begin regretting the loss of the past, which really was better in some way than now. How can you avoid creating pictures of the past or future in your mind? The technique "Right now is all I have" can help you with this. Use it every day. It doesn't take long and will benefit you more than a little. Think about your life in the present, think of the present moment, here and now, as the only one that's left in your life. You have no past, no future, only this present. Try not to apply a value judgment to the present. No matter what it's like, it *is*, it's existing right this very moment, it's alive, it's outside of time, it belongs to you, it's the most real. Don't ignore it. Accept it. You are not its source, you didn't create it, it's not your fault that the present is precisely the way it is, you are not its creator. But you are its observer.

Accept your present as if you'd chosen it. Don't create any pain, don't resist what is, but rather dissolve into it. All our sufferings are resistance to what is. And the more you identify with your mind, the more you resist. It's really the mind that resists. There's nothing crazier than denying what is, denying the obvious, denying life. Make the present – the "now" – the most important moment in your life. There's nothing more real than that. The future is rather vague, and the past is also distorted by the mind (it's the greatest minimizer and exaggerator on earth,) since the most true and real in life is only what you have now. Spend a little more time being present in this moment. Play hide-and-seek with your mind. Catch the thoughts that fly into your head. Their job is to lead you away from the "now." Don't give in; hold yourself in the now as long as you can manage. When you first begin doing this, two minutes in the present will be a record! Be in the moment of "Right now is all I have" as often as you can, totally accepting the situation. In principle, we always have two options as we move through life: to fully accept what is, or to change it, if we don't like it. If it's impossible to change what is, then it's better to accept it. Because there's nothing more idiotic than fighting what exists but which you're powerless to change. And when you do totally accept what is, then what you've been striving for so long will turn to you of its own accord, without any effort or unnecessary, senseless searching. When there's no longer any resistance and you move along with the flow, everything begins moving in your direction and working for you, because you have become a part of it, rather than a separate, isolated, suffering individual, wandering in the labyrinth of the past and the future.

The "Looking Inside" Technique

The best series is ... LIFE! I've watched 36 seasons so far, and judging by the plot, the director is a crazy person...

Make it a habit to take a look inside yourself as often as possible. What I mean is, when you're looking at something, contemplating something, it's not important what, shift your gaze for a moment to within you, as if you're flipping everything, *redirecting your perception to focus on who's perceiving everything.* Quickly, before your mind starts up, try to catch hold of what you're perceiving. Who is this? Who's doing the perceiving? Try this right now and quickly give an answer to that question. Who's perceiving what's happening?

To your amazement, you'll discover that there's no one there. There's no perceiver. Of course, if your mind has managed to slip into gear, the mind which always strives to get everywhere first and take control of everything, then the answer will be simple: **I** perceive. Of course it's me, who else would it be? But once again, that's your mind's illusion. When you first start using this technique, your grasp of the given question may be purely intellectual, but as you move forward, more and more often moments will arise in which you will have a real sense of the emptiness within and of the absence of any perceiver. Everyone has that inner silence, and at the first stage you simply need to remember that, commit that idea to memory. You will definitely get the chance to test it. It's another matter that not everyone will notice this silence, due to the mind's chatter. Although you yourself already *are* this silence. But your mind keeps you from sensing it. We attempt to do something with our mind, calm it down somehow. We try to go beyond the limits of our mind by following our thoughts or meditating or using similar techniques. But none of that is any use. You don't need to do anything with your mind. Let it play its games. Because you, your real "I", is not your mind. The technique of *looking inside* will help you become convinced of this. You can use it as much as you want. There are many things in life that we start out perceiving intellectually, there's no other way to do it. They come to us through someone. Our eyes light upon a book and, leafing through it, we decide to buy it, or we meet an interesting interlocutor, or come across a site – totally by accident – that has this or that information. And it's only later, perhaps years later, depending on the person, that you gain a practical awareness of what you once read. It's a very ordinary and interesting process, and when it occurs, at the very same time, someone will definitely be sent to be at your side, to give you hints and help you along. The teacher appears when the student is ready. For this reason, many people will see this information – that you are not your mind, you are not your body, you are unmanifested pure consciousness – as nothing more than some boring and incomprehensible philosophy that's also hard to grasp. You need only take note of it, without delving into it particularly deeply. The information will do its work at the necessary moment. For example, when I try to suggest one of these techniques to my mother, an inveterate communist and a materialist to her roots (I particularly like doing the looking inside technique with her,) she, or more precisely her ego, begins to put up such resistance that no matter how you try, she gives me nothing but "My **I** is **ME**, it's my mind, so stop asking me stupid questions." I begin laughing at the tricks her mind is playing on her and she begins laughing at me, calls me stupid and weird, says I've made up who knows what in my mind. "Someone told you this, you believed it, and now you see this silence in everything, but I won't believe all these stupid things, I have a mind," shouts my mother's ego. And let it shout, but I do know that she herself already *is* that pure and unmanifested consciousness, and that she just hasn't sensed it yet, because of all the chatter in her mind. When I learned this technique and it worked for the first time, I laughed for a long time, too, but it was at my own mind that I laughed. I want to note that you'll be able to sense the inner emptiness in the presence of an awakened person. And such a person will absolutely be at your side if that is meant to be.

As you use this technique and the "Right now is all I have" technique, you might experience sleeplessness as a side effect, because your mind will become very vigilant. It will be afraid of losing control, will be on watch 24 hours a day without taking any time to sleep. If this happens, it's a good idea to stop doing the techniques. Of course, being awake for three to four days solid is in and of itself interesting in terms of observing yourself, although it is also rather exhausting, especially if you have to go to work after being up all night.

The "Formula for Happiness" Technique

**If you want to have something you've never had before,
then you should do something you've never done before**

This is an ancient formula for happiness taken from the more than five thousand year-old Vedas. In spite of the intervening centuries, this method's magical power (although I don't like to use the word magic, it's more than fitting here) is still effective today. You'll easily see this for yourself. This method works like clockwork. Like all ingenious things, it's simple. Any person can practice it at any moment and it will always be helpful!

Only one category of people won't be able to practice the formula for happiness: inveterate egoists. They freak out at just the thought that they should wish someone happiness. A tendency to egotistical thinking, such as "only I should have all the best stuff" will not allow them to utter the phrase "I wish you happiness" even once. If you're able to say this aloud, even once, then not all is lost! ☺ Perhaps the rest of people will benefit from the other techniques I present here, such as working with dualities.

This method works on the principle of "what you send out is what you get," and this principle works because everything is united. When you sincerely wish another person happiness, you are in fact creating and radiating happiness, and so you feel it yourself at the same time. The more of it you send out, the more of it you receive.

The formula **"I wish everyone happiness!"** pronounced **aloud**, is an extremely powerful, purifying and healing technique for enlightenment, a technique that really does increase happiness. With the help of the **"I wish everyone happiness!"** formula, you purify your consciousness, your mind and your subtle bodies, eliminate ego, the sources of illness, bad moods, and problems in your relations with other. You can also wish people happiness *mentally*, but in this case the effect is not as great.

Make the wish for happiness calmly, consciously (not in a rote fashion) and as sincerely as possible. If at first you can't manage the sincerity, just do your best; the sincerity will come later, once the egoism and accumulated negativity are exhausted. Speak at a comfortable tempo, nd now and then try saying the phrase more quickly or slowly – this can affect the speed and quality of the process.

The best way to do this is to find a comfortable spot where you can be by yourself. Close your eyes and say the formula of happiness aloud. Set aside one to one and a half hours when nothing will distract you. It's better to have extra time at the end than to end up being distracted by something.

The wording **"I wish everyone happiness!"** is rather general, so it's better to begin your work with concrete people, using the phrase **"I wish *you* happiness!"** Concentrate on a **specific** person (visualize him in your mind) and wish him happiness, with the result that he begins to glow from happiness; you see how he becomes happy. It's possible that you'll have to wish him happiness **many times** before you're able to do so **sincerely**, with your whole heart, and see

125

(imagine) that he has become happy. After that, begin working on the next person. **Whenever it's possible, always speak the formula of happiness out loud.** If that's not possible, recite it in your mind, which is better than not wishing someone happiness at all.

Be prepared for the fact that your ego might resist this practice and toss out thoughts such as:

- this won't work

- don't waste your time

- don't you have anything else to do?

- how can you wish others happiness if you're not happy yourself?

- what the hell, someone else will become happier, but what about Me?

- I'm not going to wish anyone else happiness! I want happiness for MYSELF!

And so on. Your egoism will surface and dissolve into your conscious mind. There will also be uncomfortable sensations and emotions (the negative surfaces from the subconscious and disperses and disappears.) But once this you've gone through this process with even just one person using this formula, you'll get a taste of the results, and then the work will go more easily – you'll know why you're doing it. Your own experience is the best proof of the technique's effectiveness. Remember that it's precisely **egoism that keeps us**

from being truly happy. Egoism and happiness are mutually exclusive.

What's best of all is when you yourself fully understand what true happiness is. **True happiness** is not one pole (polarity) of a "happiness – unhappiness" duality. It exists outside of this duality. Real happiness is not a fleeting external pleasure. It has an internal nature – Understanding your true essence. And when you desire this very type of happiness (Understanding, Awareness, Liberation, Enlightenment,) then that produces a stronger effect than the desire for the happiness of temporary external pleasure. If it's hard for you to grasp this, do the best you can, while maintaining the core principle: you sincerely wish someone happiness and see him grow happy. You can imagine him breaking into a smile, being joyful, or shining from the happiness that fills him to overflowing.

When you begin wishing others happiness, your ego might put up a fuss, because the ego doesn't like this. You'll have to get through this by repeating the phrase "**I wish you happiness**" *over and over again.* Sometimes this can take a long time. As we work, we observe our thoughts, accept them for what they are, after which our ego weakens and quiets down. Carry on this way with each person you're working with.

The most difficult thing is when you wish another person happiness in the form of enlightenment. The ego senses that if this person becomes liberated and happy, then it won't be able to play its usual games with him, the games that sustain it. For the ego, the end of these games means disappearing, dying. Imagine that all your relatives, friends and acquaintances became liberated and happy. It's not possible to control them any more, push their buttons, use them to your own ends, or make them wrong, unhappy, force them to sympathize with you, and so on. They are fully free and happy. What do you feel? If you have **unpleasant** sensations or thoughts, it means… you have work to do.

Many people ask, how long should I work with a given person?

The End Result

- you're able to **sincerely** wish that person happiness, without any discomfort

- calm, relaxation, tranquility

- a feeling of lightness, liberation

- inner joy, happiness or bright positive emotions

- pleasant bodily sensations (rising energy)

By the way, you can successfully use the formula for happiness to smooth over relations that have soured, or to free yourself from unpleasant situations others create for you. Work on your relatives, close friends, friends, colleagues, boss, etc., in other words, everyone with whom you live, have frequent interactions, as well as those who have had a big influence on you in the past (particularly if it's a negative influence.) When you master the formula for happiness, work diligently on your enemies (those people who would be the last ones you'd think of wishing happiness!) When you finish working on specific people, it's fitting to practice the formula in a general way: "I **wish everyone happiness!**". This is a practice for every day. You can use it no matter what level of development you're at, at any time of the day, and combined with anything else you're doing. Even wishing someone happiness just mentally is better than allowing your mind to chew over some mental garbage for the thousandth time, or, even worse, digging up something negative. **Make up your mind first thing in the morning to enter into a positive flow and hold onto that mood all day, to the extent it's possible – and you'll be amazed at how quickly your life changes for the better.**

The more you practice "I **wish everyone happiness!**" the more focused you become on happiness. And what you focus on is what you receive. When you wish everyone happiness, people begin thinking better of you, because **there's a connection between people on the level of thought, or soul.** People sense what others wish them. And they alter their attitude to you accordingly, as soon as you begin wishing them happiness. It couldn't be any other way. As you practice the formula "I **wish everyone happiness!**" you'll notice results fairly quickly, and the more often you send others happiness, the more happiness will appear in your life. Problems will begin to resolve all on their own without any worry or effort on your part.

Try it and be happy!

The "I wish everyone happiness" technique (repeating this phrase) works on the level of thought. Next comes the level of action – real actions in the physical world that bring other people closer to happiness (which should not be confused with temporary pleasure.) But this is a more complicated level of interaction, and at this level it's important to distinguish between actions related to bringing others happiness and actions aimed at indulging someone, at entertaining the ego, at being obsequious, and so on. Because when a person is trying to please someone and offers every possible kind of support and help to another person only so as to not seem bad or do something wrong, then before long, in the best case scenario all he'll receive is a kick in the butt (this is the origin of the proverb "Don't do good to people, and you'll know no evil.") In the worst case, he'll develop an illness that will clearly point to problems in his approach to life.

The "Gratitude" Technique

Just for a moment, imagine what our world would be like and whether it would even exist, if the Creator had, even for a moment, doubted he was acting correctly.

This technique is appropriate for absolutely everyone, even children. Of course, a hardened egoist will immediately pronounce it a technique for chumps or something like that. One day when I was on the bus someone lifted my wallet from my purse. I discovered it was gone when I got to work. Right away I used the gratitude technique, to which my colleague remarked ironically, "There's nothing to do but resign yourself to the situation." You don't feel like admitting you're a chump, but you also don't feel like going to the police, so the simplest thing to do is to turn to the gratitude technique; it's just perfect for chumps who sit slack-jawed on buses. By the way, not long after this, the proprietary emblem on my colleague's car was stolen, and he grieved for a week afterwards, and only some time later did he calm himself down and say, well, okay, I'll buy myself a new emblem. In other words, he unintentionally employed this very same gratitude technique, but not until much later, when he'd already managed to blame himself for not setting his car alarm, for not putting the emblem inside the car, for parking in a dangerous spot, etc. In other words, after becoming royally entrenched in his mental garbage, he ultimately made his way to the gratitude technique without even intending to do so. And so, I encourage you not to lose any time blaming yourself and rather, to use the gratitude technique I'm going to tell you about in all cases. However, using it does not entail fully capitulating to life's events. Change what you have the power to change, fight for your rights, hold your ground in stating your point of view, punish wrongdoers – for punishment, as an element of education definitely helps people cultivate their soul – but when you do it, do it without becoming entangled in the process, without a desire for vengeance, without a sense of personal superiority, and absolutely, use the gratitude technique.

After an unpleasant life's occurrence, take a look at it from the point of view of "It's all God's Will." For example, something happens, say, some unpleasant event, and you understand that it's God's Will. At first your understanding will be intellectual. Later you'll get a deeper understanding of the processes that are taking place. If you have a reaction to this event, if you shout, curse, blame someone else – that's also God's Will. Something seems unacceptable to you – that's God's Will, too. If you accept your unpleasant situation and calm down – that's also God's Will – you "unstick yourself" from what happens and stop seeing yourself as a participant in it and turn into an observer (an impersonal witness) of God's Will. This is accompanied by the disappearance of the illusion of the **I**, and your entanglement and the illusion of your **personal** command of the situation also disappear. The illusory sense of oneself as an autonomous (independent) being, as the author (source, creator, doer) of what's happening also disappears. The sense of guilt, the illusion of freedom of choice, regret about what's happened – these disappear. All that remains is the witnessing of God's Will.

As you practice the gratitude technique, use phrases that seem the most fitting for you. Definitely feel them. Mechanically repeating the sentences only moves the air and won't lighten your state at all. You need to fully feel and agree with that you're saying. You can use the phrase: *"**Thank you, Lord** (Life, Consciousness, Being, choose the one that fits your belief system, culture or views,) **for everything that has been, is and will be, for every minute I've lived, for all that remains for me to experience. It is all your Will."** This will bring you closer to total acceptance of what is and free you from egoism and its negative consequences.

"It's all God's Will" is not simply an interesting theory, not a trick or a means of calming oneself down. It's a useful practical instrument that speeds our development. Judge for yourself. When you move away from accepting that all is God's Will, that you have absolutely no freedom of choice, then you grow weak. At any given moment, all that happens is what should happen at that moment, so what's the point of needless anxiety? If it's not possible to change anything in what's happened, then the best state to have is that of being present and observing the Games of Our Consciousness.

When you have a dream, you generally see all that happens in the dream as no more than the mind's games, and you allow these games to play out without trying to change anything in them. You accept everything just as it is. It's just the same in "real" life, which really differs very little from nighttime dreaming, until such time as a person attains enlightenment and wakes up.

Pain and Suffering

A devout beggar makes this request: "God, please make it so that if I come upon someone else's property on the street, I'll have no desire to pick it up." God thought a moment, and rewarded him with back pain.

Is it possible to escape pain and suffering? This falls into the category of philosophical questions. Nearly all spiritual teachers say that pain and suffering are nothing but illusions conceived by our mind. Of course, we enthusiastically believe this, but that doesn't make things any easier for us. We continue to experience pain and suffering throughout our lives. So, a purely intellectual grasp of the fact that this is an illusion, and that suffering does not exist, will not help us. At this stage, those are just empty words. People continue to suffer, fall ill, and depart life in tragic ways. Grief brings massive emotional pain to all who encounter it. When I was first beginning to practice, I went through a period of heightened awareness of reality. I cried when I watched the news. A plane crashed. On the television I would see the relatives of the victims and I'd cry right along with them. When someone would explode with rage in a school classroom and go on a shooting spree, killing other students, I'd again cry and not get it, how can you kill people like yourself: after all, in shooting them, you're shooting yourself. As I became more skillful at not identifying with my mind and my emotions, this period of entanglement in what others were going through was replaced by sympathy, but without becoming entangled in what was going on. It would be wrong to say that I've become more cruel or less sympathetic, but I no longer cry. I have the understanding that this is the way it's supposed to be, that there's no other way it could be, that this is the natural order of things. The same goes for pleasant moments in life, too. There's no entanglement in them. The majority of people might feel that when someone is in this state, he's depressed, he isn't interested in anything and has no emotions. Actually that's not the case. Many of my friends began labeling me in various ways, thinking up various names for my "mental illness." But in reality, I was healthier than ever before.

So, pain and suffering. The main source of any physical pain, of our sufferings, of the unpleasant occurrences we experience, our life's tragedies, is emotional pain. It appears long before any real unpleasant event arrives on the scene. Identifying it can be very difficult. It settles into our body unnoticed and begins destroying it from the inside out. It's like a cancerous cell: the quicker you draw that pain out from inside you and destroy it, the less likely it is to take full possession of you. Where does emotional pain come from? It is all of our fleeting, even miniscule dissatisfaction with situations, our irritation, feeling of guilt, jealousy – in other words, our resistance to objective reality. All of this nourishes our emotional pain, drop by drop. Once it reaches certain levels, it begins to act, through the mind, of course. It can drive some to suicide, some to illness, still others to insane acts of aggression. Emotional pain is quite tenacious. Once it's settled into your body, it's capable of dozing there for quite some time without any feeding at all. You just won't notice it's there and it will wait for a convenient moment to remind you of its presence. Sometimes all it takes for the pain to wake up and get to work is one cross look or a phrase tossed out randomly. And if you also nourish it with unpleasant situations and dissatisfaction, then this pain will very quickly enslave your entire organism, erupting like a volcano, in the form of both physical and emotional suffering. Don't forget that all human emotion – no matter whether it's positive or negative – feels the need to be experienced over and over, constantly. Emotional pain is no exception, it needs as much pain as possible in order to live, it needs energy, for it will perish without it. For this reason, people begin attracting the kind of situations that are necessary to feed the pain sitting inside them, and they do it unwittingly, influenced by their thoughts. Thought feeds the emotion, and vice versa, and on and on, endlessly, these two pals romp together, totally controlling you, and very skillfully, too. Because you attribute all of this to yourself and think that you're the one in control. It's complicated to break free of this vicious cycle. You can tell yourself all you want that you won't shout any more or blow up, you can take classes in anger management, and in managing depression, etc., but the emotions come out on top again and again. I've met people who could sit and meditate for an hour, but if someone suddenly burst into their space, they would totally lose it. And the person was unable to do anything about it. Many might pose a reasonable question. If we can't do anything with our emotions, then why pay them any mind at all? But if we don't keep track of our emotional pain, don't give any attention to our emotions, then one can easily become the kind of life long sufferer who finds that everything in life always goes wrong. Many people don't even notice how much they build things up in their heads, and then when something really does come crashing down on them, then all they do is ask, why me? I really am unlucky, right? Of course, the person himself really does not want to suffer, but what's facilitating the suffering is the emotional pain that he himself created. In order to break the cycle of suffering (and I'll note that there is suffering which simply does exist, necessary sufferings that we do not cause ourselves, but these are few in number, the majority of them are designed by the mind) it's necessary to track your emotional state each day and not allow emotional pain to take control of you. The question is, how can you do that? Many people take the idea of tracking, observing and not allowing emotions to control you to mean that you should control and squash your emotions. It's impossible to squash them. Let them come out, but each time you do, you need to see and observe them. Be an independent outside observer. Not a judge, not an expert, just an observer. What takes place at such a moment? When you see that what's come up is envy, wrath, anger, jealously, greed, which are all one and the same, by the way – then recognize that these are your awakened emotions. Fix your attention on them, sharpen your gaze, be present with them. Now you know they're inside you. That they are living alongside you and aren't just some quiet residents, but also make their "voices" heard now and then, go on the rampage. Well, it's you yourself who let these residents in long ago, because you were unaware, you gave them a little room and allowed them to latch on and suck away at your life's energy, so now you have to live with them. Remember that. See that you possess these emotions. Observe them every time they appear. Many people who blow up easily, because of their nature of their personality, see nothing reprehensible about exploding with anger.

Meanwhile, fury, anger, ill-will, envy and jealousy are always destined to flow into pain and suffering, only later on.

If thoughts arise about being good-for-nothing, about how unhappy you are, how empty your life is, how quickly the years have flown by, how quickly you've grown old and the like – that's once again a sign that you are not present in this moment, that your emotions have once again taken control of you. The second you stop watching your emotions and become one with them, when you identify yourself with your mind, i.e., when there is no observer – at that moment, your emotions become the master and you their slave. Emotions are like mercury – they can craftily slip away from the observer, masking themselves, hiding, merging with the observer. If they manage to do this, then there is no longer any observer. There's only someone who's shouting, or pounding on the table, a wrathful representative of the class of homo sapiens. We become our emotion.

The first textbook I used to help with managing emotions was Uspensky's book "The Fourth Path." The author wrote that all you need to do is catch sight of an emotion at the moment when it's taking you over, and it will immediately retreat; what's important is to catch sight of it. In actual practice everything ended up seeming a lot more complicated. In a moment of fury or maliciousness, I could see my emotion very clearly. I saw myself from a distance, saw myself shouting, being mean or hysterical, but it was impossible to stop myself. First you let off steam, and only then do you begin to analyze things. Years of work on my emotions were required before they backed off. Therefore, if you can

138

see your emotions but still can't do anything with them, that's totally normal. Let them come out, but as they do, don't stop watching them. The main thing is to not give up the observer, or, as I usually call it, to "hold the center." It's always easier to follow your thoughts. But with emotions... it's not so simple with these little bugs hidden deep within you: they catch you, sometimes unawares, and always just at the moment when there's no observer present. The contemporary teacher of Advaita Cesar Teruel loves to say at satsangs, "Don't lose sight of the seer while you're seeing." Don't allow your emotions to encroach on your freedom, don't make a slave of yourself. That's the sole way to free yourself from suffering. Watch your mind and your emotions. Always be with them, but don't be them. That's the path to freedom from the mind's slavery. But observe without evaluating, judging, digging around in them, analyzing. The link between emotions and thoughts will gradually weaken. They won't feed each other so actively any more. The witness, the observer, will stand between them. So, suffering will transform into awareness. And awareness accepts everything, since awareness itself is everything.

Illusion as an Obstacle

**No matter how far removed someone is from
any philosophy,
he nonetheless has a theory or article of faith
that explains why he lives the way he does,
and not some other way.**

Our illusions cause no small share of our suffering. They spawn incorrect thoughts. These thoughts in turn elicit unhealthy emotions. Emotions lead to illnesses, and illnesses to unhappiness, disappointments, etc.

Where do these depressing thoughts come from? From our illusions. After all, we're convinced that things should be precisely *this* way, not *that* way, and that this is the right way. We have articles of faith in our head, our set ways, boundaries outlined in red, and when we go outside them, we feel depressed and guilty. We go outside them in any of a variety of ways, often even unwittingly. Only ridding ourselves entirely of these illusions will lead to freedom. Including freedom from suffering. Our illusions keep us from progressing in our spiritual development and are a great hindrance in the process of coming to know ourselves.

Unfortunately, knowing what all our illusions are will not free us at all from their abundance. Otherwise, everyone would immediately rid themselves of their illusions and become enlightened. Nonetheless, it's very useful to take a look at our illusions from time to time. Let's start with the most central illusion: "I am someone." The identification in our head, i.e., equating ourselves with something or someone, causes a separation between ourselves and the world, sometimes even opposition to the world. This illusion gives birth to still others. "I act as a separate mechanism, I am an isolated being, I exist fully on my own, I need no one, no one loves me," etc. All of this comes out of the illusion that I am someone. "I'm cool, I'm smart, I'm famous, I'm a doctor, I'm a professor," or, on the other end of the scale, "no one loves me, I'm unlucky, I'm useless, I'm sick," and so on. But one way or another, everything originates in the "I." As long as our "I" exists, it will always be separate from the world, and this division will create more and more new illusions and suffering. When a person reaches a certain level of development, then the identification, the equation of self with one's "I" disappears. What remains is just the knowledge that "I am." I simply am in this world. At such a level, even gender distinctions are no longer felt as strongly as they were previously. There's the understanding that you are the same as I, you are the same pure consciousness as am I. You are I, we are a single organism in the universe. At this level, you fully grasp the profundity of the Sufi saying: a monk knocks on pilgrim's door, and in answer to the question, "Who's there?" replies, "You." At this level of consciousness there are no illusions.

Another significant illusion is our imaginary freedom of choice. As soon as we do something wrong, we begin regretting what we've done, experience guilt, and berate ourselves. And we do the same thing even when we happen to do something successfully. We puff up with pride and joy, we beat our chests and take credit for everything ourselves. But really, in both cases, we simply acted as we were obliged to act. Nothing personal and nothing extra. We simply could not have acted otherwise. Why do two people in identical situations behave entirely differently? Because one of them gets it into his head to do one thing, and the other would never conceive of acting that way. And this has nothing to do with each person's upbringing, personal sense of responsibility or even his conscience. Even if you tell someone, "You can't do that," or "That's wrong," he'll do it anyway and won't think it's at all the wrong thing to do. Each person acts in accordance with his own nature, his own psychological, biological and genetic conditions. Even two children raised in the same family by parents who love them both equally will react to their life's situations in different ways. But the problem here lies not in how we react, but in our belief that we're the authors of our actions. Externally, of course, we are the authors, but only conventionally. We choose how to act, and often we spend a long time considering things, having doubts, collecting advice, but in the end we act the way our nature dictates. We simply cannot act any other way. For this reason, our conviction that we act freely brings us uncertainty, doubt and anxiety. We begin choosing how to act, we're always mulling things over – should we do this, or would that be better? Even when we're standing in a store, we size everything up, think it over, although what we'll buy is known beforehand: we'll buy precisely what we're obliged to buy based on our worldview, tastes, life experiences, goals and so on. We simply cannot buy anything else. It's a big illusion to think that we can do something that departs from our nature. Our nature does everything itself, through us. So, it's useless to beat ourselves up over some wrong actions, steps, and mistakes. Overall, the topic of how involved we are or aren't in this process always elicits lots of debate. When people of various religious orientations get together at our house in the course of long winter evenings over a cup of tea, it's always the Christians who debate particularly furiously. They are sure that people always have choice. The choice of whether to go to a restaurant or to church. The choice of whether to travel the narrow path bequeathed to us by Christ, or the wide path. The choice to observe a fast or not observe it. The Buddhists usually keep silent. But the fact that one person goes to church while the other goes to the casino is all determined by one's internal constitution. Both places are equally wonderful spots for spending one's free time, but in the heads of two different people, they'll be perceived as mutually exclusive. For the churchgoer, the casino is the devil incarnate, while for the casino regular, the church is tedium. It can happen, of course, that a fan of casinos ends up in church, and vice versa, but that will be determined by one's natural tendencies, too.

One more illusion that delivers no small amount of suffering is the illusion of knowledge. We know how things should and should not be. If something goes wrong, we know that this should not be. In reality, all our knowledge, our rules of behavior, our images of what's right and what's wrong, exist only in our head. They didn't turn up all on their own; rather, they were thrust upon us long ago by society. If the illusion is built on comparison – that's the way it is for him, that's the right way, the good way, but things are different for me, and that means they're wrong and bad – then that's an illusion constructed by your mind, a mind thirsting for benefit. But who's thirsting for benefit? The "I" which definitely appears as someone. That's what suffers, too, as it becomes overgrown with unnecessary feelings, emotions, anxieties and illusions. As the philosophers say, everything is an illusion, including life itself. However, I wouldn't call the manifest world an illusion, because after all we see it, sense it, recognize it, exist in it, and we can see the total interconnectedness of everything in this world. It's only our "I," which exists autonomously, (for which there are reasons of it own) that sees itself as a separate being lacking interconnectedness with consciousness. It's that "I" that is a total illusion. Dispelling this illusion is a complicated matter, since unmanifested consciousness is hidden from us. But it's for this purpose that we live on this earth, to dispel illusions and move forward. This brings to mind the wonderful words of Eckhart Tolle: "You are here to realize the Divine purpose of the universe – to **unfold.** This is how significant you are. To come to know yourself as Existing outside the thinking ego, as the peace that stands behind the mental noise, as the love and joy that stand behind pain – this is what constitutes freedom, salvation and enlightenment."

The Brevity of Thoughts

A rule of hygiene: never think the same thought
twice.
- Emile Auguste Chartier

It seemed right to me to spend a little time talking about one crucial element of our constitution – our thoughts. It goes without saying that everyone's thoughts vary, depending on how they live their lives. But the difference lies in mainly in our thoughts' practical nature, in their contents; the thought process itself is identical for everyone. We differ from each other in the contents of our thoughts, their quantity and in the speed with which we think them, but the nature of the thoughts, how they arise and play over and over, that's the same for everyone. Everyone replays in their head the conversations they've had with others in the course of the day, dialogues they've composed and are planning to give voice to. We all think alike. We draw comparisons, some of us more than others. We think about whether we're living right (by the way, even maniacs think about this. They know they're living wrong and think about that, but can't do anything about it. Just like many of us, by the way.) We burden ourselves with things that seem significant to us (we all have our own collection of these.) We analyze our lives and others' actions. We come up with this or that theory or philosophical system and attempt to explain our experiences with their help. We attempt to stuff our own conceptions of life into these systems. If our conceptions coincide with the conceptions of a given religion, then we become followers. We seek knowledge that will make our lives easier. And finally, we all want something, and because of these wants, new thoughts keep arising over and over. Our wants feed our thought process. We call all of this life.

However, no explanation of life and no philosophical system will make man's existence easier for him until he stops rummaging around in learning. It's not difficult to find an explanation for any life's event. You can even find a great number of explanations for any one event. Each philosophical system will explain it in its own way. But does that make things easier for the person in question? What does it matter that he knows the reason something happened. Will that really soften the effects? There's nothing more idiotic than taking this advice: find the reason, correct it, and you'll change fate. A person won't find anything. He'll wander lost like a blind kitten, armed with others' learning, while at the same time not accepting fate, and wanting to change it for the better. And you can run around in circles your whole life in search of a reason, and miss out on your actual life.

Once you've travelled a rather long path searching for causes and effects, studying philosophy and religions, searching for yourself and the reasons for your actions, then you gain an understanding of the uselessness of the knowledge we glean from various sources. It is all something borrowed, incapable of either changing us or making us happier. I don't mean practical scientific knowledge, born with the help of thought – this type of knowledge really does make our lives easier. I'm talking about the uselessness of philosophical and religious knowledge. Unless you've tested it on yourself, this kind of knowledge can throw you off track, enlist you, frighten you, enslave you. Only through the process of observing yourself can you come to discover the source of your problems.

Thought in and of itself is designed to work *for* a person and help him function in this world. But in fact, a person becomes the slave of thought. He fully bends to its will. We need thoughts only in order to survive in this world. That's the full extent of their role. Everything else that arises in our head has no practical significance. A genius creates a masterpiece without even thinking about it. An artist paints on a canvas, but at that moment he doesn't exist. What I mean is that there are no thoughts. It's the hands themselves that mix the paints and give birth to the masterpiece. Mediocrity – mediocrity does think. I often find that after I've written one of the chapters of my book, I reread what I've written in the morning and don't recognize my own words. Who wrote this? People think a great deal. They think about every thing on earth. Thoughts give birth to words. People talk a great deal, too. Often about nothing at all. Emigres in particular talk a lot. Evidently this reflects the fact that they aren't able to speak enough in their native language. They say so many empty words. And that's only a small proportion of what's in their heads. In actual fact, the nature of our thoughts is brief, just like everything in this world. A thought flies into our head and out of it. It's impermanent, just like everything around us. But we want continuation and permanence. That's mainly because we fear death. Permanence, even if it's only in our heads, only if it's the constancy of an isolated incident, gives us a sense that the entire world is permanent. But there is no permanence in the world, never has been, and never will be. For this reason it makes no sense to pay the thoughts in our head any mind, latch onto them, play out whole screenplays of events. All of that is an empty and harmful pastime. A thought is brief, but when we latch onto it, we cause a giant tangled lump. The mind is a great exaggerator. With the help of our thoughts, we can create and think up anything we want, and then suffer because of it. The reason for thinking lies in desires. We are always wanting something, usually comforts (material, mental, emotional,) and that's why the thinking starts. If we want nothing from the world, there will be no thinking. But that doesn't mean there will be no thoughts in our head. They'll be there, but they'll be brief, and there is a higher blessing in this. Children are very interesting in that respect. They have only brief thoughts in their heads. Thoughts fly in and out of their heads, without being held there at all. Because children live for today, they don't have long-term plans or desires. Everything is minute by minute. They are blessed. Adults desire more, which means they also suffer more. Thinking is harmful for the body, since it elicits conflict (after all, the body needs so little, and the head always needs so much.) Neurasthenia occurs. In addition, aging proceeds much more quickly in people who think a lot. The best anti-wrinkle cream is a peaceful head, even an empty one, I'd say. I speak from experience. One shouldn't latch onto one's thoughts. They are always in our heads, it couldn't be otherwise – they'll cease only when we die. But we shouldn't expand them into thinking. Brief thoughts won't hurt anything. They aren't capable of taking possession of you; they serve you and not the other way around. The best way to become happy is to simplify your life. But we're constantly complicating it. In America there are two words that open all doors you come across: "pull" and "push." These are the only two words to use for opening and closing doors. But we keep thinking up more and more words and options. That's how thinking is born in our heads. I recall a funny story on this topic about a university rector who invented an apparatus to count thoughts. He takes his apparatus and goes to some students to see how well it works. He goes to a future manager and says, "Hit me," and at the same time he looks at the apparatus. The student thinks, "If I whack him, all kinds of problems will come up: they'll kick me out of school, I won't get a refund on my tuition, my parents will be all over me, I'll never find work. No, I'm not gonna hit him." The rector goes to the law department. He says to a student, "Hit me." The same scenario. The student thinks, "Problems will start, hooliganism, criminal statutes, I'll ruin my career. The best case scenario is that I'll be fined, but I don't care about the money. No, I'm not going to take his bait." The rector goes to the philosophy department. The very first student gives it to him good. The rector immediately checks the apparatus. It's silent – no thoughts. The rector doesn't give up. "Can you hit me again?" Without a moment's thought, the student whacks him again. Again, not a single thought. The rector is very agitated. Well, there has to be something in this student's head. "Can you do it one more time?" At this point the apparatus finally shows a thought has occurred: "Maybe I could try using my foot."

By the way, in spite of philosophers' complicated theories about matter and existence, they in most cases tend to lead simple and unpretentious lives.

Thought is not long-lasting. That is its nature. But we keep on thinking, because of the knowledge we've acquired about ourselves, about the world, about how things should or shouldn't be, about how they will be. We keep thinking good thoughts because we like to keep reliving something good over and over again. We feed our bad thoughts by thinking about how to avoid this or that, about what will become of us now, and so on. But in reality, any thinking is useless. It's not capable of solving a problem, only of tangling it up even more. What solves problems is correct action, and that is always spontaneous. The only goal of thought is to serve the body. But we come at things from the opposite direction. Thoughts are capable of making our bodies sick, of wringing us out emotionally, squeezing all the life out of us. Not feeding our thoughts means learning to live more spontaneously, without long-term plans, flowing with life's current, rather than against it. Thoughts are primordially short-term, unconnected. It's not complicated to return them to their natural state. But in order to do this we need to not feed them. We don't need thinking. Life is always impermanence, a vector constantly changing its direction. Trust this vector, and don't try to manipulate it. And then you won't ever need to think the same thought twice.

The Path to God

Faith is understanding the meaning of life
and
Recognizing the responsibilities that flow
forth from this understanding.
– Tolstoy

Why does one person reflect on his destiny, while another doesn't? Why does one person take unbelievable steps to develop his consciousness, while another doesn't even have the slightest inkling that he could do this? One person makes unbelievable sacrifices, turns his back on life's pleasures, lets go of earthly delights and heads for Tibet in search of eternal peace, at the same time as another person doesn't even know that such peace exists. Each person possesses his own level of soul development and his own needs. And need will always trump any desire, for it's more powerful, since it comes not from the mind, but from inside. By the way, it's been noted that those who are on a spiritual path are less satisfied with life than those who aren't engaged in this search. It's possible that it's precisely these difficulties and dissatisfaction that nudge one toward the eternal, to search for oneself, toward self-expression. However, it's not entirely true that a person who wallows in earthly desires is any happier. As our observations show us, this happiness is in any case transient, and a dark patch always comes along to replace a light patch. For this reason, sooner or later, through suffering or without it, everyone will find his way to this search. This reminds me of a certain parable:

A man goes to the barbershop to get a haircut and a shave, as usual. He gets to talking with the barber who's working with him. They talk about various things, and then suddenly touch on the topic of God.

The barber says, "No matter what you say, I don't believe there's a God."

"Why not?" asks the client.

"Well, it's totally obvious. All you need to do to be convinced there's no God is to go outside. Tell me, if there's a God, then why are there so many sick people? Why are there latchkey children? If He really did exist, there would be no suffering or pain. It's hard to imagine a loving God who would allow all of this."

The client thinks for a minute, then decides not to say anything, rather than get into an argument.

When the barber finishes up, the client leaves. Leaving the barbershop, he catches sight on the street of an unshaven man with overgrown hair. (He seems not to have had a haircut for an entire eternity, that's how scruffy he looks.)

The client goes back into the barbershop and says to the barber, "You know what I'll say to you? Barbers don't exist, and no matter what you tell me, they don't exist."

"How can that be?" the barber asks in amazement. "What? Don't I count? I'm a barber."

"No!" the client cries. "Barbers don't exist, because otherwise there would be no unshaven people with overgrown hair like that man walking along the street there."

"My good man, this has nothing to do with barbers. It's just that people make the choice not to come to me..."

Why don't they come? Because it's not yet the right time. If you go around with your hair overgrown and you like yourself that way, what do you need with a barber? You'll find you have need of one when the right time comes for you to reconsider what's important to you.

In general, the topic of who comes to whom – God to man or man to God – always causes debate in philosophical circles. Believers tend to suggest that really, it's man who comes to God and more often than not comes by way of suffering, bad luck, illness and similar messes in his life. Esoterics tend to assert that it's God who comes to man when he's ready. But whichever way it happens, this doesn't play any significant role in finding or discovering God. I'm more of the mind that God really never leaves us. He's always with us, it's just that man himself closes himself off from Him, closes all the gates, constructs giant dungeons and mazes around himself, and he can't see anything beyond this. But when he suddenly discovers that he's empty, then it turns out that it's not so simple to get out of the dungeon, for the gates have managed to rust shut, and besides, he's grown used to the darkness. What's new, there beyond the door, frightens him. Many people prefer to stay locked up that way in that dungeon where the mind is king, and they don't allow any love to make its way inside. After all, an old, familiar friend is best.

But if a person suddenly grasps the fact that he's in a dungeon, then until the day he dies, he'll never stop trying to make his way out of it, even if his attempts always end in failure. The need to escape will take precedence over everything, including a comfortable life, comfort, and terror. And this will happen sooner or later. Liberation will definitely come.

Love Conquers All

**Love is the swiftest thing on earth. When it comes,
you don't see it coming, and when it leaves,
you can't catch it.**

It happened once that some souls had come together before incarnating onto Earth.
And so God asks one of them:
"Why are you going to Earth?
"I want to learn to forgive."
"Who are you planning to forgive? Look around, see how pure and light and loving these souls are. They love you so much there's nothing they could possibly do for which you'd need to forgive them."
The soul looked at its sister souls and it was true, she loved them unconditionally, and they loved her in the same way!

154

The soul grew sad and said, "But I so want to learn to forgive!"

So another soul comes up to her and says, "Don't be sad, I love you so much that I'm prepared to be right there with you on Earth and help you experience being forgiving. I'll become your husband and I'll cheat on you, and drink, and you'll practice forgiving me."

A different soul comes up and says, "I also love you very much and I'll go with you: I'll be your mom and I'll punish you and meddle in your life any way I can and keep you from living a happy life, and you can practice forgiving me."

A third soul says, "And I'll be your best friend, and at the worst possible moment I'll betray you and you'll get practice at forgiving."

Still another soul comes up and says, "And I'll become your boss and because I love you, I'll treat you cruelly and unjustly, so that you can have the experience of forgiving."

Yet another soul offered to be a mean and unfair mother-in-law...

So, it ended up that a group of souls who loved each other gathered together and came up with a script for their life on Earth geared toward experiencing forgiveness, and then they incarnated.

But it turned out that on Earth they had a very difficult time remembering who they were and what their agreement was. The majority of them mistook this play as real life, and began growing insulted, getting angry at each other, totally forgetting that they themselves had composed this script for their lives and that, most important, they all loved each other!

We have way too little love in our lives. And also too little common sense that would allow us to avoid being drawn into this game we call "life." We don't have enough love to see all that happens to us as an excellent, flawlessly planned script. This script's director has only one task – to make us better, which means turning a frightened, sometimes malicious half-animal with issues and an underdeveloped soul into a kind, wise, loving being called Man. We all want to be the director of our own lives. That's why we suffer when the actors suddenly stop playing their roles according to our rules. We suffer because we don't love these actors. How can you love someone who not only doesn't play by your rules, but who also often even acts against you? This is how all manner of manipulation, mind games, illusions, empty expectations and life's crazy disappointments come into being. We even play these games with those at home, and without even realizing we're doing so. And what about outsiders who just happen to cross our path? At times we're prepared to trample them in the dirt. Even if we observe social niceties on the outside, terrible things can go on in our head at times... and all because love is lacking.

A certain negative tendency has appeared of late. Because people have grown a great deal through their spiritual searching, they've become more interested in the meaning of life, in spiritual knowledge, and as a result, their spiritual ego has become noticeably more puffed up and has grown in size, while at the same time, their level of spiritual development has remained the same. This lack of correspondence between the level of the soul and the mind is now more evident than ever before. On the primitive level of everyday life, this leads people to continue to treat each other terribly, but what's different now is that the behavior is explained through reference to secret doctrines, as karmic ripening, by beautiful words about the necessity of suffering, etc. Not long ago, one of my acquaintances, who happens to be highly developed in the area of philosophical questions and esotericism of the individuum, filed suit against his mother. To my mind, it was a trivial matter. When I expressed my amazement, my acquaintance replied, very convincingly, "There's a cause and effect connection here, it's a karmic ripening. I really love my mom, but learning comes through love, and through me she's gleaning a life's lesson and transforming her consciousness." Very intelligent and contemporary, and you can't figure out what it means. My diagnosis: an extremely puffed-up ego lacking in love. My acquaintance used a couple of ironclad arguments gleaned from the latest smart book he'd read. And in our times, there are more and more people like this, people whose mental capacities – for a variety of reasons – have not yet undergone change, but whose heads are crammed full of spiritual knowledge. I see sadness in this situation, since people are not moving forward in their search. And what's more, they continue treating each other badly, while calling themselves "teachers," while educating others and extending a helping hand to them. And people like this are so strongly convinced they're right that they're prepared to stick with it to the bitter end, because this right course is supported by book knowledge which they have read but, unfortunately, not tested on themselves. So much more benefit is brought to their own souls and others' by people who might not have read even a single book their whole lives and have never even heard such intelligent words as karma and consciousness, but who have done so many loving acts that it just melts one's heart to hear about them.

How do we cultivate love in ourselves? By giving. But by giving not in order to receive, and not so that we become good in our own or others' eyes (which is also the same result,) but in order to bring joy to ourselves and other people. You can even give a passerby a smile, assuming, of course, that you have one. But how can you muster a smile if your mind is digging around in the past or focused on the future? In that case you won't even notice the passerby, you'll blow on past him. How can there be any talk of a smile then? It's hard to give something away if you have nothing.

A wonderful love "accumulator" is forgiveness. To truly forgive means to forget forever. When we forgive, we're not only lightening our own state, but also practicing loving, first of all ourselves, because in forgiving others we forgive ourselves, for consciousness is united. All these separations into yours, mine, ours are only in our heads and they exist only while the individual consciousness is awake. In practice, it's not simple to forgive fully. It's easier to pull this off if you've already accumulated some reserve of love, and it's nearly impossible before a person has learned to love. But this is a feedback loop. If we forgive, we won't have to wait long before receiving a new serving of love. And vice versa – when we don't forgive, we lose all the love we've accumulated.

One of my colleagues and comrades in this work, instead of asking, "How are things today?" prefers to ask, "How are you doing with love today?" At first the question seems absurd. How can you gauge love, how can you measure it so you can tell whether everything's all right in that department? Because it's not some substance you can place on a scale and measure. For example, when your head hurts, you can definitely say your head is bad today. But what about when you're talking about love? How can you define your love reserves? Actually, on the level of everyday life, a good indicator of an abundance or lack of love does exist. It's infallible in determining someone's inner state. An indicator of love for each day is a person's energy level. When there's enough love, there will be a surplus of energy, there will always be time for everyone and everything. When love is absent, strength will diminish. When there's no time, there's no love. There's only one time this love-measuring thermometer can malfunction – when a person gets caught up in a game, when he's been drawn intensely into something and is fully under the power of the mind, because he wants to win this game at all costs. Then there will also be lots of energy, because there's motivation. But this type of energy will fade quickly, since there's no love behind it. So, asking how you're doing in terms of love today is much more logical than asking the dry question, "How are things?" Love is the daily giving out and receiving of energy. Things will go well if there's energy. A person will be sick if he doesn't have enough energy. A person dies if there is no energy left at all. You'll easily agree that this is true if you observe life. If a person stops giving out love, preferring to just receive, then he'll remain healthy a little longer, because the laws of the non-material world are more static. He might feel perfectly fine right up until the moment he exhausts all his reserves. Then the ailments or problems in his life will start. In some cases, the process of losing love drags out over the course of years. In others it plays out more quickly. But the final result is always the same – as soon as a person stops accumulating love, his soul no longer has anything to do on earth. The death of the great 19th century poet Pushkin – who died after an idiotic duel when his poetic powers were in full bloom, at the peak of his popularity – has always puzzled me. D'Anthes' wild bullet ended the life of one of the most talented people of that age. A poet died from a wound which now isn't even considered dangerous and can be cured in the course of a day. But if you analyze his life, particularly his last years, there's no doubt that had he lived, it's unlikely that he would have written even two new lines. He did all he could and needed to do. So, from the esoteric point of view, his death makes perfect sense. It's possible that his further presence on earth would have been pointless.

I always compare being in love with heaven on earth. If you observe people in love, it's easy to be convinced that they're in heaven. They don't need anyone, nothing worries or torments them. They're high. It's also a fact that this state quickly passes, again due to incorrect emotions, jealousy, greed, desires, ambitions, pridefulness, a thirst for new adventures and other attributes foisted on us by the mind. What happens is that we ourselves cast ourselves out of heaven, repeating Adam and Eve's steps over and over again. We confuse love with pleasure, pride with pridefulness, sex with instinct. When a person falls in love, he's carried off into heaven. But, unfortunately, because he doesn't know how to love, he just as quickly ends up being cast out of it – even though heaven is already here, on earth, right here and now, accessible to anyone who is open to love. Let us love each other and find heaven on earth each and every day.

A Letter

Regarding seekers:
A hedgehog is walking along and suddenly comes
upon a stream.
He throws himself into the stream, swims across it,
walks on...
He gets to wondering, hey, can hedgehogs swim?
He goes back to find out – and drowns.

I decided to publish the letter of a certain seeker, a letter that struck me as interesting from the point of view of self-inquiry. I think that to some extent it reflects the thought process of many who are searching for truth.

"The very words 'self-realization' or 'enlightenment' present us with an interesting situation. I totally agree with and accept everything that the masters and gurus of all stripes write about this, but either I'm not understanding something, or else I haven't matured enough, but each time I encounter an "enlightened being" on my life's path, or read the next book on this topic, then each time I find that my state, my consciousness, differ from the state of those people. I begin projecting their words and find that I don't feel the same range of colors inside, the same peace, stillness or stillness that's so beautifully expressed in the books and interviews. And so naturally, the sense arises that they've discovered something that I haven't yet discovered. Even if you take such basic concepts as freedom, acceptance, or love, then here, too, there's a certain defectiveness of the individual "I", compared to the total freedom, love and acceptance that's mentioned in the books of the enlightened ones. What really "gets me" are the spiritual experiences and

experiments of individuals who have "become one with being" in the course of meditation, who have grasped the illusion of the "I." I understand that the mind can give birth to any experience whatsoever, that there's no point in any of it, but all the same, the "I" keeps seeking. And the critical approach to your own existence, in which you're still not experiencing silence, and in which storms blow through, that view itself keeps you from giving up the search. If this state of complete silence is possible for one person, why is it impossible for someone else? And if it's possible and – what's more – we already possess it, then why don't I sense it, why don't I have the profound peace, quiet, awareness, unconditional love, the present moment... I could keep on listing... Do you see that simply knowing that I am enlightened doesn't make me so? I know God is within me, I am divine, a part of being... but in my case this is only intellectual knowledge, gleaned from someone else's experience. There's knowledge, but no sense of it."

It seems to me that many people's main problem is that we don't accept what is. Or rather, we don't accept turmoil, and we crave silence. In this context, enlightenment for us is like a lifeboat. We'll attain it and get what we want: eternal peace, stillness and silence. I can tell you with absolute certainty that all of that will come only upon death. So why strive to attain this so early. That's one thing that we'll definitely attain. So enlightenment can wait, and meanwhile it's better for us to live, right here and now. And what really is truly necessary is total acceptance. We can have that right now, this very moment. And to do that we don't need any special preparation or knowledge. Accepting what is, means accepting everything, including the lack of sensations, silence and peace. It's accepting everything that is, the way it is. And really, enlightenment is nothing more than a certain mental construct, a certain word that expresses something, and to which there's no point latching on. You can say that we're all already enlightened, and that's accurate. And you can say that no one can be enlightened while they're alive, and that's accurate, too. The Buddha also said, "If you meet the Buddha, kill him, for that's not the Buddha." There really is no person who lacks an "I" at his core. So you can just not worry about that at all. And as concerns what others say about their divine experiences, meditative states, spiritual searches and enlightenment, well that reminds me of a joke: A little old man, 78 years old, comes to a psychotherapist, who asks him what's bothering him. The little old man replies, "Well, it's like this, I have such bad luck, for the n-th time I couldn't do it." "Well, what're you gonna do," the doctor says, "it's your age." But the old guy won't lay off and goes on about how his neighbor's 84, and that neighbor says he can do it. Here the doctor gives him some ingenious advice: "Well, so tell him the same thing. Who's gonna check?"

So, the only one you can trust is yourself. As far as the so-called practices go, the ones I've introduced in this book, they'll definitely make your life easier, as will many other things, such as alcoholism, or religion, or Advaita's kind ideas, or the concepts of the enlightened ones. But the best option would be to just forget all of it, including all the practices and the very idea of enlightenment and this book, and accept what is, including your inability to forget. It is so marvelous to live when we cast off all that's unnecessary, when the mind doesn't challenge us to "grow", to attain something, to develop, to seek, when we accept everything, including our inability to change anything. Everything!

Afterword

The first people to read this book were two friends of mine, a kind couple, and the first thing they said was, you can't do this, you've totally revealed yourself, you're selling your innermost secrets, writing about your personal life. Why do that? They suggested I delete certain sections in the first part. I tried doing that. But the act of cleaning things up, editing them, seemed dishonest to me. I wanted to be totally honest with my readers. This is my life without any window-dressing or things left unsaid. This is my path, which I fully accepted and came to love. I really would like it if my life's example helped someone find their way, establish true priorities. Because you really can learn a little bit from others' examples. And if the methods I introduce here bring even one person closer to a more conscious perception of life's events, then that means my scribblings are not for naught.

To my presentation of the methods I'd like to add the note that they don't represent some direction that you can follow that will necessarily bring some kind of result. It's impossible to follow each and every thought, impossible to be constantly practicing, impossible to receive something before it's given. At some stage it will be useful to just forget everything you've read, throw all your books away, relax and enjoy your life. All will come in its own time. More precisely, you already have everything. True, there are people who can't bear idleness, so-called goal-oriented people. They always have to be doing something, for some reason, just so they're not sitting idle, because otherwise they start to feel bad. It's possible that after working with some of the techniques, these people will lose heart, for they're

165

the ones who always need to get something, attain something, they need an immediate result. In that case, for them, it's better to focus on the body. Give more attention to physical acts, take better care of the body, indulge it, spoil it. You can start with sports, which is a wonderful way to take care of your body. You can also choose one specific part of the body and pay more attention to it for a specific amount of time, look after it aesthetically. For example, for a month focus on making your hands beautiful, spoil them with this or that skin-care product. Later you can shift your focus to your hair or to something else. Jumping around in this way can distract you from searching for yourself in this world. In principle, everyone can benefit from paying this kind of intense attention to their bodies, the same way they'd look after their mental constitution. Because when all is said and done, it's the body that serves as the sole doorway through which anything can open up to us. You need to love yourself as much as possible and never skimp on yourself. Only by loving ourselves will we also be able to love others. When we don't love ourselves we start nagging others to love us.

As for me, my schooling in love is ongoing. Each day is full of new subject matter that brings me one tiny step closer to Being. The world around me changes daily, and my own worldview changes along with it. Now I know for sure that when there will be enough love, I'll definitely be able to bear a child. At least now the doctors aren't as categorical in their diagnosis as they were before. However, love's presence, just as its absence, as well as everything in our life, is depends fully on the will of God Most High. And all we are doing is learning to accept it gracefully.

I would be happy to have readers share their responses with me at lifewithloveasitis@gmail.com. If questions arise about putting any of the methods into practice, I'm ready to help. My wish for all people of our planet is that they will part ways forever with envy, money-grubbing, greed, jealousy, ill-will, dissatisfaction and illusions. Of course, will they want to part with you? But it wouldn't be a bad idea to replace them with love, grace and joy. I wish everyone love and peace.

This book expresses the author's opinion, and it doesn't claim to present authoritative truth, for each of us himself attains his own authoritative truth.

I'd like to express my gratitude to all the teachers whose books served as guidebooks for me. These are the works of Osho, Gurdjieff, Rudolf Steiner, Dzhiddu Krishnamurti, Gopala Krishnamurti, Eckhart Tolle, Samael Aun Weor, Wayne Liquorman (Ram Tsu), S. Lazarev, Lise Bourbeau, Viilma Luule, Ken Wilerber, and the notes of Cesar Teruel. I'm particularly grateful to the people I have encountered on my life's path. They have all, without exception, including my parents, served as my Teachers at various points. I haven't always had smooth relations with all of them, but each one has done and continues to do his part in helping me learn life's lessons. I'm especially grateful to my husband, who has been particularly heroic in travelling this entire path with me.

A separate BIG THANK YOU to Susan Downing, without whom this book would not have turned out the way it has.

And to end with, a joke:

"How are people who pray in church different from those who pray in a casino?"

"The ones in the casino do it mu-u-u-ch more sincerely."

May our prayers always be sincere, no matter where we are when we offer them.

Here are some books I'm preparing for publication:

"Our Little Ones. A Few Games for Parents, *or* A Delightful Upbringing"

"The Metaphysics of Pleasure, *or,* Sweet Quagmires", dedicated to alcoholics, gamblers and others who live life in the fast lane.

▪▪

TABLE OF CONTENTS

www.ingramcontent.com/pod-product-compliance
Lightning Source LLC
Chambersburg PA
CBHW051758040426
42446CB00007B/428